A FIRESIDE BOOK

PUBLISHED BY SIMON & SCHUSTER INC.

NEW YORK • LONDON • TORONTO • SYDNEY • TOKYO

BRIDGE OF LIGHT

LAUNA HUFFINES

Fireside
Simon & Schuster Building
Rockefeller Center
1230 Avenue of the Americas
New York, New York 10020

Designed by **Diane Stevenson / Snap • Haus Graphics**

Manufactured in the United States of America

10 9 8 7 6 5 4 3

Library of Congress Cataloging in Publication Data

Huffines, LaUna.
  Bridge of light / LaUna Huffines.
    p. cm.
  "A Fireside book."
  ISBN 0-671-67089-1
    1. Spiritual life. 2. New Age movement.   I. Title.
BL624.H84   1989
131—dc19   88-30467
                                                               CIP

CONTENTS

ACKNOWLEDGMENTS

I want to acknowledge my gentle and loving guide, Jaiwa, who is the real author of this book.

I want to express deep gratitude to Sanaya Roman and to Orin, her guide, who saw the need for this material to be made available to the public and were behind this book's conception; to Barbara Gess, my experienced and intuitive editor, whose light-filled vision and support made this book possible; to Bob Harlow for his cheerful optimism, skills of the electronic world, and literary perspectives; to Dr. Marcelle Kardush, a great friend of this book, who made many valuable suggestions; to Dr. Kardush's graduate psychology students at San Francisco State University for their helpful responses to these tools of light; and to Elaine Ratner for her fine editing on parts of this book.

My gratitude also goes to Angelia Robberts and the Wisdom Synthesis Group of the Los Angeles area, who have held a steady focus of light upon this book; to Ed and Amerinda Alpern for their heartlove; to Marilyn Clevenger, who faithfully transcribed and typed much of this manuscript; and to Dr. Duane Packer, for his generous support.

I would also like to thank Dr. John Enright, Viviana Carball and Peggy Thompson for their comments as early readers; Dr. Linda Johnston, Linda Bandino, Dr. Kathryn Ridall, Scott Catamas, Loring Greene, Debbie Davis, Sandy Hobson, Frank Korn, Ruth Ross and Jerry Haas, Evalena Rose, Heather Preston, Shirly Davalos, Heidi and Bobby Bass, Wendy Grace, Trudie London, Lorraine Osterer, Joy and Chet Watson, Rosalind Whitney, Donna Hale, Mark and Annie Susnow, Emily Ivy, Arman Simone, Kathy DeLucia, and all the people in my classes who are demonstrating the power of the tools in this book through their own lives.

My special thanks to my parents, Wren and Sam Caudle, who were my earliest teachers of living from love; and to my sons and their wives—James and Jane, Ray and Ann, Phillip and Holly, and Donald and Mary Catherine—whose deep spiritual convictions take many forms.

I also acknowledge with gratitude the loving support of all my wonderful friends who have patiently waited many months for me to be free to play with them again.

To you who are the healers, teachers, and leaders in integrating these new frequencies of light throughout all life.

FOREWORD BY SANAYA ROMAN

I first met LaUna in 1983 through a friend who wanted me to meet a wonderful woman who was teaching classes and writing books. She was also interested in meeting Orin, a guide I channel, and soon we had set up a meeting. Little did I know I was about to meet a friend who would change my life.

During our first meeting, Orin talked to LaUna of the importance of the work she was doing. He told her that she would channel a series of books that would teach people how to work with light and other esoteric techniques. These tools would allow people to create what they wanted more easily, align with their higher selves, and manifest their life purposes. Orin told her that a very high guide had been working with her for many years to prepare her for this work, and that she would be channeling soon.

Several months later I had the honor of being present when Jaiwa (pronounced Jii-wah) made his first appearance. Jaiwa's presence had been growing more apparent to LaUna during the writing of her book, *Connecting,* and she knew she was ready to make a verbal connection. Orin held a focus while Jaiwa began to speak and greeted him as an old friend. The energy in the room was wonderful; I felt Jaiwa's presence as waves of compassion and love. Meeting Jaiwa was a very uplifting experience.

Jaiwa explains that he is here to assist us in discovering and carrying out our world service—our higher purposes and the special contributions we came to make. He provides ways to bring our personalities into alignment with our higher selves, giving us wisdom, courage, and power. Jaiwa's gentle, loving, and penetrating insights guide us to love and value ourselves and to trust our visions and paths.

Jaiwa gives us tools of light that open up new choices for us. These choices allow us to feel more joy and give us the power and freedom to manifest our dreams. The wisdom he presents assists us in expanding spiritually and gaining a greater mastery over our lives. The number of people coming to work with Jaiwa both individually and in classes continues to grow dramatically. These tools of light have made such a difference in people's lives that Orin and others asked LaUna to make Jaiwa's work more widely available. I am happy that Jaiwa's love and guidance are now accessible to even more people through this book.

It is a joy to work with Jaiwa and LaUna. I have the deepest respect for both of them. My friendship with Jaiwa has greatly enriched my life, and LaUna has been a wonderful example of how to live a life filled with light, laughter, and true caring for others.

FOREWORD BY ORIN

Greetings from Orin! I am honored to introduce Jaiwa, a being of light filled with compassion and love. He is a teacher and spiritual guide, and we have much respect for him in our realms.

You may be feeling the higher vibration of energy and light that is pouring into the planet during these transformative times. It is no longer a question of bringing in more light but of understanding how this light may be affecting you and learning to use it to grow spiritually and create the life you want. Jaiwa is here to teach you tools of light you can use to work with these new energies, and this book lays the foundation for his work. He gives you many processes, techniques, visualizations, and words of love to assist you in having more joy, inner peace, self-love, and loving relationships. These are the tools of light we use in our dimensions to create results, and they do work.

Using these tools of light will greatly accelerate your spiritual growth and personal transformation. They will enable you to stay calm and centered, follow your higher vision, and increase your vibration so that the world you experience is more positive and loving. Whether you are a novice or very advanced on your spiritual path, these tools will help you awaken a deep inner knowing of how things are done in the higher realms and how to create the life you want more rapidly and joyfully.

The application of these tools is infinite. You can use them to improve an important relationship, or to discover your life purpose and to create a higher future. You can use them to launch your business or career and bring yourself opportunities and contacts with people who will help. You can use them to balance and stabilize yourself, create more inner joy, and flow with the universe.

Jaiwa is here to empower you to awaken to your greater potential; open your heart; and become more radiant, alive, and vibrant with the light of your higher self. You will feel Jaiwa's love and compassion as you read this book, for he is here to show how to have the best life you can imagine and recognize the beautiful person you already are.

INTRODUCTION
BY LAUNA

You may be drawn to this book because you are feeling ready to express your unique wisdom and abilities in the world. You may be opening to more light than ever before as you meditate or connect with your Higher Self, and finding that your life is getting crazier instead of easier. Or perhaps you would like to create loving, supportive relationships and sound a new note of truth and compassion.

You may already be experiencing shifts in awareness, seeing yourself and your life from a greater perspective, even glimpsing other dimensions of your existence. Disillusioned with the ability of most formal religions or gurus to guide you into more light, perhaps you have started breaking through barriers of the smaller self and celebrating the guidance of the larger self. Perhaps you feel overwhelmed with how to integrate all the new understanding you've gained from your Higher Self and you want to do so while remaining balanced and sane.

Whatever your motivation to read this book, you can use the spiritually energized Tools of Light presented here to live from a wiser and more compassionate vision of yourself and others as you move toward your visions and goals. The principles and tools in *Bridge of Light* will help you create a sacred place in which to experience the true divinity of who you are so that you can express a new dimension of love and wisdom in every part of your life.

My own amazing journey into light began one evening in the spring of 1962 after I had put my four small sons to bed and was meditating in a quiet room of my home. That evening I imagined a cloud of pure light moving toward me—so powerful that it would absolve all of my mistakes, even those I couldn't remember. Never in my wildest dreams did I anticipate what would happen next. I suddenly found myself in the midst of a very clear but blinding light. I was fully conscious, but without a physical body, completely stunned by an overwhelming presence that permeated me and all of the atmosphere. Virtually every belief I had about what was true or real dissolved in one instant. Then I became terrified of dissolving into that light forever, and I struggled to get back and feel the weight of my body against the chair. I had unconsciously expected that such an intense spiritual experience would be filled with beautiful colors, celestial music, and perhaps a few angels and palaces, but there were no colors, boundaries, buildings, angels, or even people in this brilliant light.

An entirely new world had opened to me. Everyone and everything seemed to blend into one grand design. When a spider met my gaze and stood motionless for a timeless moment, it seemed that I was a part of the spider and he was a part of me. I experienced such a tender and deep love toward everyone I saw that I wanted to reach out and touch each person whose face revealed sadness or suffering. When I looked into another person's eyes, especially my children's, I could see the light of their souls shining forth like a star.

But the more I meditated, the crazier my life seemed. It was like living in two separate worlds. The bliss and peace that I experienced in meditation seemed remote when dawn broke each morning to signal the beginning of another day of commitments. No matter how busy I was, though, in the back of my mind was the awareness of that one moment of being a part of a great light.

I realized that these higher frequencies of light needed to be contained with proper grounding, just as electricity does, and that there must be ways to gently bring in the light as needed rather than be swept off balance by too great a charge at once. But I had no idea how to do that.

Twenty-five years after my first experience of light, I began to receive a gift that I almost rejected because it didn't fit in with my beliefs. I was writing my first book, *Connecting,* when I felt an intuitive impulse to stop writing and to "be still and listen." Finally, information and ideas began streaming into my mind— from a different frequency than my own soul. This connection felt like a stream of energy moving through a specific point at the top of my head, whereas the connection with my own Higher Self or soul always felt like a gentle sensation of openness all around my head.

When I turned to this source a tremendous compassion would flood my body and emotions, a compassion that reached far beyond all of my metaphysical concepts of it.

I do not experience bringing this energy into my mind as a trance but as tuning to a specific frequency in the airwaves, just as one tunes to a specific radio station. Some days the reception is clearer than others. I can censor or interrupt at any time. Occasionally I may attempt to finish a sentence that is being received. If I am slightly off the mark, there is a pause in the reception and then a gentle correction.

I usually have a simultaneous awareness of two different viewpoints, the other frequency and mine. The first is based on a wider perspective; mine is filled with practical experience from many years of teaching and counseling. At almost any moment I can tune to either one or both.

I knew immediately that I was receiving from a source far wiser than myself, but I did not want to fall into the illusions that come so easily when one gets involved with channeling and can lead to questionable claims about the source. Perhaps this source was simply another part of my own Higher Self or soul; perhaps it was a pool of humanity's collected knowledge, or a specific archetype such as described by Carl Jung. Or could it be that I had been allowed to tune to a group of advanced souls working from another dimension to assist humanity? For months I analyzed what this source of knowledge could be. Finally, I decided to *accept the information based only on its merit, not on where I or anyone else believed it was originating.*

This source is called "Jaiwa" (which translates, I was told recently by an Indian scholar, as "the celebration of breaking through barriers").

When friends have asked Jaiwa's identity, he said:

"I am a teacher from a gentle race of beings that does not quarrel, does not fear, and has free choice moment to moment. We are creators on our plane, just as the human race is learning to create consciously upon your plane.

"In the center of the world we stand—not the world as you know it, but the world behind form as you have known it before birth and will know it after death. This formless world is with you now, yet because of the illusions and distractions of human sight and sound, you may only sense it at times.

"We reach you through the soul's sound within the heart. We have no physical boundaries, although we can focus our energy, or parts of it, into any time or space and be present there. I am here to help you reach the God within and without. Focus not on who we are, but on our message."

Many people heard about this source and began coming for individual sessions with Jaiwa. As soon as I tuned to the frequency of Jaiwa, I could see them through different eyes—and was immediately immersed in a profound awareness of their souls' beauty. Jaiwa showed me how all of us are awakening beings of light and then showed me how to help others see who they are.

People responded so dramatically to Jaiwa's field of energy that I began to teach these principles and tools to groups in weekend gatherings. In these groups we felt our physical bodies filling with new energy, our emotional selves becoming calm and positive, and our mental selves focusing to see more clearly. We realized that we were being transformed very rapidly.

Friends wanted this teaching in a book for handy reference. Jaiwa soon gave me a title and an outline, and I began to write. He made it very clear to me that this book was to be a cooperative effort. Jaiwa was to provide the broad concepts and insights; I was to add practical applications when needed. So each chapter contains Jaiwa's wisdom and also input from me, usually relating specific experiences that people went through.

Some chapters deal with material that I was familiar with before starting this project, and some contain material that was new to me. Some I was frankly skeptical about. Once our group applied the information, and saw how we changed into far more confident, compassionate, and wiser beings, we were convinced that Jaiwa was here to awaken us to new levels of purpose and joy—and that these beings knew exactly what they were doing.

Bridge of Light explains Jaiwa's principles for integrating into your life the intense spiritual energies that are now available. It demonstrates how to use this new power to live from higher purpose and experience joy as you expand. Each Tool of Light it presents can help you achieve a finer and more harmonious balance. Each one is simple and easy to use. I have been using them in my own life, and I have opened to a clarity, direction, and creativity that I did not dream possible a few years ago. Friends, clients, and students who are using these tools are having similar results. Most important, we are discovering the ease of loving, forgiving, laughing, serving, and receiving that is possible when we know how to integrate this light into our lives.

Every chapter presents practical tools to build your Bridge of Light, or Rainbow Bridge. Building this bridge is the necessary process to balance the spiritual energies in any land or language. Without it, the intense frequencies that we contact in meditation may completely disrupt our lives without any benefit to us or our work.

Bridges of Light are not a figment of the imagination. Each one consists of actual streams of spiritual energy that can be directed into any part of your life. With today's highly developed minds and intellects, bringing patterns of pure light into your life is simpler, more direct, and free of old superstitions. These new patterns of spiritual energy bring clarity, wisdom, joy, trust, and love, or humor—whatever is most appropriate for each person.

Not only can you receive tremendous energy from these higher qualities, you can send these same blessings directly to others and watch relationships change and evolve into higher ones. This book will show you how to spin strands of light from your own heart to each spiritual quality and how to share that joyful, energizing reality with everyone you know—even with all humanity.

A WELCOME
FROM JAIWA

I bring a hearty welcome to you who have volunteered to come in this time of accelerated spiritual growth. I am here to telepathically transmit to you a very important message: A new and intense energy is spreading throughout the atmosphere of this planet. It will be experienced as an inner note. The sound is silent, inaudible to ordinary hearing, but quite clear as it vibrates within the center of the soul. It strikes a resonant chord, echoing again and again among the people who are sensitive to it. Many are responding and joining this call.

This note proclaims a higher frequency of light on this planet, far more than has been available to humanity in the past. It comes in response to the sincere prayers and desires for peace that have been offered in people's hearts from every part of the planet, and brings great opportunity for everyone who is prepared.

The more rapidly people learn how to balance and integrate this higher frequency of light into their lives, the more easily they can absorb and expand with it. Even the highly evolved among you may not realize at first how much is happening. Doubt, discouragement, or confusion might temporarily wash over you, but as your mind becomes accustomed to the finer vibration, be prepared for a new recognition of your divine nature. Illusions of helplessness will begin to dissolve, along with the sense of isolation or loneliness. Opportunities will be unlimited for profound joy and great, healing love to be given and received.

Here's what you can expect. As this energy hits the planet, it shakes up all that is not of the higher vibration. The degree to which people hold onto those things that are not of the higher vibration is the degree to which they will experience pain. Misunderstandings and hurts from the past will be surfacing to be healed. Powerful new tools to handle people's fears will be needed.

Nothing can remain the same in this heightened intensity of awareness. In your personal life you may already be discovering that trying to hold onto anything that isn't working causes disturbances. If a relationship is not assisting both people to expand in some way, this can't be ignored any longer. Your work or career may seem pointless. Or you may have noticed that habits of careless bookkeeping, risky ventures, or vague hopes that "everything will work out" now call for your precise and clear thinking.

In addition to business transactions, even friendships that you once could let slide may need attention. Some of the ways things were always done (which created pointless guilt) may seem silly to you now. You may also be finding the need to let go of other obligations, such as activities and projects which have no intrinsic value to you.

Since the new energies are so friendly, and bring in abundance and success, many people will get what they want. Their challenge will be to learn how to handle success. It can cause more anxiety than the feeling of lack that preceded it. Handling what one is accustomed to can seem easier than change.

Great opportunity means great intensity. This is a time of extremes. Nothing happens halfway. On the days when you feel good about yourself, you can move like the wind using currents of energy to propel you faster. When you feel bad about yourself, you can be prepared to use your new tools of light with precision and move into healing currents of greater understanding. You are probably already seeing many new and higher ways to respond to people and situations.

So much is happening that you may be learning to drop everything that does not fit into your higher purpose, simplifying your lifestyle so that you can take pleasure in moments of your life this very day rather than driving yourself mercilessly after an ideal that is not close to your heart.

You may be more sensitive to emotional suffering, not only that of your family and friends, but of all humanity. As your heart opens to this new force of light, you may feel a deep compassion for people who suffer from poverty, lack of freedom, or ignorance. It can be tempting to try to deny that feeling, or to go back to how you once thought or felt. You may want to get away from it all, to find a cave and just be peaceful. But as tempting as it may sound when you are confused or overloaded with responsibilities, retreating isn't the answer. Enlightenment doesn't happen in a cave. It happens as you reach out to love yourself and others equally. You can begin to manifest a wonderful life step-by-step—beginning now.

If you are contemplating ways to live from the authority of your Higher Self instead of others' expectations, you are already responding to these energies and are in the first wave of its force. The light waves don't move by geographical location, but affect the most sensitive and aware people first.

In the inner crises approaching, what will be needed and valued more than any other skill, knowledge, or gift will be the ability to receive with accuracy the messages from the Higher Self or guides. To make this connection, each person must build his or her own Bridge of Light. Every person builds these bridges out of the substance of the heart's desire.

A variety of powerful experiences are going to be brought to you by your higher consciousness. At times you may be awakening to a deep sense of ecstasy and bliss that resides within you. Even experiences you don't enjoy will bring a gift with them, helping you to trust your Higher Self and its wisdom. Each experience prepares you to move into a grander dimension of yourself. Every thought or feeling of a lower vibration brought into the light can release you into true freedom.

This energy reveals new dimensions of who you are—morning and night, thinly disguised in a person, a situation, a dream. What you think is not light may be truly light. Light comes disguised in many costumes and characters. Watch for the moment of recognition when you can say, "Ah, I am seeing and understanding from this new frequency of light. My confusion is only temporary. Here's how I can float on this wave and become the master." In this way you can watch every experience become a clearer reflection of the beauty of your soul.

The next wave may be one that will carry you to an even higher point of vision. By being prepared for it and seeing its gift, you will know how to jump on its crest and ride, balanced by your confidence, and exhilarated as you adjust to its changing flow—moment by moment.

You may be thinking of changing your lifestyle to allow more time for being alone as well as with people like yourself. Kindred spirits are gathering into informal groups in every town and city of the world, sharing insights and knowledge. Now is a good time to seriously consider the location where you feel happiest and which is most harmonious with your sense of purpose. A harmonious place to live is coming to be more valued than a higher-paying job in a less harmonious location.

The brighter light does not just take you to a vague mystical state that makes you feel good. It alerts you to what is happening on the larger scale, and gives you the clarity to make choices that bring every part of life into a finer attunement with the light. As you sense how to integrate these changes, you may see ways to share your gifts—new understanding, love, wisdom, truth, humor, and joy—with all who can receive them.

If you have had some of these realizations, you are already opening to these energies more fully. If you want a more powerful Bridge of Light to higher guidance, or are searching for a higher purpose, you may become a part of the growing group of teachers and healers for humanity. You teach best by making your own life work through manifesting what you need to express your true self and demonstrating the joy and abundance available by the authority of your Higher Self.

By the time these energies hit in full force on this planet, you can be in a position to assist many to awaken to their God within as you honor *your* highest understanding and wisdom. Having come through the same experiences that others are facing, you will have learned how easily unconscious fears can get stirred up—and how to dissolve them in the light. You will have seen through the glamour of being overattached to another person, to a "relationship," or to a career. You will have learned to balance your emotions with your lighted mind. Your power to assist will come from your delight in the adventure of life.

You do not need a special kind of education or background in metaphysics in order to understand and use the tools of light presented here. You don't have to be religious, but simply aware that a higher source has conceived and created the basic structure for this planet's system. We shall show you how to bring your life into harmony with the forces of light and to stay close to your soul and its guidance, not only when challenges come, but also when life is easy, giving you more than you could have asked for.

Think of yourself as a mountain climber of the mind. Let the flaming spirit within you mark the path as you go. You have nothing to fear, and nothing of true value to lose. The next step is to make preparations, for not even the most skilled mountain climber would attempt to climb without his equipment tested and in place. Some of your equipment has been stored or forgotten, but it is still there. Each chapter will show you how to build a lighted body and a lighted mind so that you will be able to use and direct the greater light that is pouring into your life from the higher energy field of your spiritual Self. You are ready to create and use new tools of light—polishing the facets of each one so that it may transform whatever it touches.

We invite you to use these tools so that your inner light can reveal what has previously been hidden: the wondrous dimensions of your wisdom and your spirit of love. Your guide's love and mine are with you as you read this book. Take what is useful and resonates as truth to you and use it to rekindle the flame of your inner knowing. The transforming power of this book is not only in the words but in the energy of light that pulses in and out as you read.

HOW TO USE
THIS BOOK

*B*ridge of Light is divided into four sections. Section I, "Temple of Light," takes you into a special place that has been prepared for you by higher forces of light. You develop new breathing rhythms to slow your brain waves and then practice receiving and sending messages using the higher mental and soul frequencies from the telepathic room of your temple.

Section II, "Bridges of Light," shows you how to spin a Bridge of Light from the substance of your heart to the highest soul qualities. You tap your spring of joy, pervasive love, and courage within the vast palace of your superconscious self, and you learn to synthesize several soul qualities at once, such as trust, truth, compassion, and confidence.

In Section III, "Creating a Soul-Infused Personality," you discern the difference between your personality and your Higher Self or essence goals, get acquainted with each side of your personality, clear your energy field of negative emotions, handle present challenges through the power of a finer frequency of light, and change any unwanted memories of your past— maintaining your sanity and balance all the while. You practice infusing each part of your personality with the soul qualities you brought to yourself in Section II.

In Section IV, "Assembling Your Highest Possible Future," you will be using the tremendous energy that has been freed in Section III to actualize your purpose, choose freely from the authority of your own Higher Self *how* to do this, and practice energizing your physical body with light. In this section you consciously sound a new note in your life that reflects the light and beauty of your being. You can delight in the adventure of integrating and using all the light you have contacted to create with higher purpose.

An exercise is provided at the end of most chapters to help you practice using your tools of light to create your happiness and success. Do the exercises only if you feel like it. You will get value from the book simply by experiencing each exercise as you read. Some people may prefer to read the book first and then go back and do the exercises that fit their needs. Or you can stop reading as you go and do each exercise before going on to the next chapter. Each experience can build on the next one. Read this book from any level you choose. Once you go into your Temple of Light and learn to spin a Bridge of Light, everything else is optional. Choose from your heart's wisdom.

There are several ways to use the exercises. You can make tape recordings of your favorite exercises so that you may enjoy them in a relaxed state with your eyes closed. If you prefer to hear them in another voice, I have recorded several of them for your convenience. (Refer to the Appendix and Additional Resources in the back of the book.) Or you can meet in groups and have someone read the exercises as the group goes through them. Choose what works best for you. Soon the habit of using each Tool of Light will become automatic, and you can do the exercises in your imagination very quickly at breaks during the day. If you get a notebook and record your insights and inspirations, the results of your exercises, and your goals, you will gain an extra benefit. Reserve a special section for your telepathic sending and receiving, and you may be quite surprised to see how accurate and precise your work is becoming.

Very likely you will find ideas here that validate what you are already receiving from your higher guidance. Your openness to receive new light and to use the knowledge revealed creates a line of energy that deepens and widens the channel through which all of us receive from our Higher Self and guides. The questions you ask come to me when I sit in the special place to receive. Next, I tune to the channel through which Jaiwa comes in and wait to receive the solutions and answers. Consider yourself a contributor to this book if it answers some of the questions you have been asking or opens doors for you to step forward into your own work and tremendous worth in this world. I acknowledge your contribution and your presence with deep gratitude.

If you read *Bridge of Light* from your luminous temple that you will visit in Chapter 1, you can double the value of this book. Jaiwa encourages us to relax into a new rhythm of breathing, thinking, and feeling as we open to receive more light at this critical time—the greatest moment in the history of the awakening human spirit.

TEMPLE

OF

LIGHT

Thﬁis section gives you a pure and clear space to go to for inspiration, wisdom, and loving understanding. It leads you to the discovery and exploration of a beautiful temple filled with luminous light. This temple is your own, created for you by the higher forces of the universe and energized by many high beings. This sacred space helps you to recognize the incredible power of your own soul and to work with your own guide. You will learn about the power of your breathing rhythm to slow your brain waves and to assist you to enter this temple wherever you are. In the last two chapters of this section you will explore your crystal-domed telepathic room for receiving messages from higher sources and will learn ways to send important messages of healing and love to people anywhere on the planet.

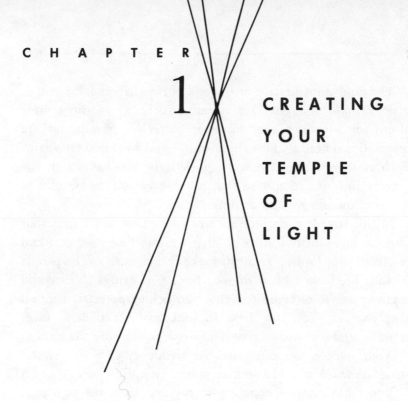

1

CREATING
YOUR
TEMPLE
OF
LIGHT

JAIWA There is a place that exists on an-
other dimension of reality. It is a highly energized place that has
been created by the higher forces of the universe. It is energized
by many high beings who are holding a focus of light on it day
and night. This place is your Temple of Light.

We who are serving as guides will show you how to reach
your Temple of Light. This temple allows you to be in a very
pure and clear space where you can create whatever you want.
When you start creating from the higher planes, it is important
that you are in a clear and pure space so that your light work can
be done without your being affected by denser energies. Your
temple helps you to rise above the density of the earth plane so
that you can create and receive impressions from your soul in the
pure energy of the light.

The guided meditation at the end of the chapter takes you to your Temple of Light. Just imagining being in the temple aligns you with its higher vibration. After you have been there once, all you need to do is think of it—and you are there again. Each time you begin to work with light you can sit in the protection of the temple so that it can give you the benefits of its vibration of love and healing light.

In this temple you can empower your vision and bring your purpose more easily into your life. You can heal your past and re-create your future. You can make connections to the people in your life from a heart or soul level that brings in new and higher patterns of being together and being appreciated for all that you are. You can draw in soul qualities such as love, courage, and joy, and receive clear impressions from the guides. In your temple you can raise the frequency of your cellular structure and heal and energize your physical body.

You can transmute negative energy and move through your crises and challenges with greater joy and ease. You can understand your own feelings and see how to get all your emotions to support you and your higher purpose. The compassion that flows through you when you are in your temple is all-inclusive; you want each person you know (and all of humanity) to enjoy great peace and happiness.

All the tools and exercises in this book will be far more powerful when you use them in this temple. Beginning with a new pattern of breathing, every technique for creating your highest possible future is enhanced when it is brought into the energy of your temple. Here your mind is free to see new choices, to conceive new ideas, to tune to the greatest minds of the planet and to the higher guides.

With the waves of light coming in, now you are being given an opportunity to understand yourself, your source, and your life from a new perspective. From the moment you make a connection with your soul, God within, Higher Self, or essence, you are on your path. When you enter your Temple of Light and open to the energy there, you are connecting with your soul. The temple is the soul in a symbolic form, loving, protecting, teaching, and illuminating you.

In the future the most valued prosperity will be the prosperity of consciousness. In your Temple of Light you will be able to experience an infinite number of expanded states of consciousness. It is a place of bliss and ecstasy, and the more you align with it the more you will automatically move into these expanded states.

You can shape the electromagnetic particles of reflected light to mold this temple into a form of beauty and light that match the images of your Higher Self. It is a sacred place, different for each person. The grace of its design is created by your own pictures of the most beautiful and joyful images you can imagine. Crystalline structures, beautiful music, lush gardens—all are created by your imagination.

There are no limitations to what you may find or build in your temple. It can be a temple of amazing splendor and beauty, shimmering with the light of your God or your Higher Self. Its energy will become more powerful each time you visualize it. Gradually your connection will be stronger until you can move in and out of the temple very easily, even when you are with others.

Each time you enter this temple and sit inside you may experience it differently. The ceiling may become like a cathedral, or you may discover an open skylight for the sun's rays to shine into your temple. Sometimes it will be very quiet; at other times you may hear the clear sounds of bells tinkling in the garden, or chiming from somewhere within your temple. Different fragrances may waft into your temple, each a very subtle essence of flowers or herbs. The walls may become more luminous, as if lighted from within, changing from alabaster or marble to amethyst to clear crystal—or they may even disappear. You may find other rooms that are there for special purposes.

LAUNA I *go into my Temple of Light many times each day to connect with my soul's love and wisdom as well as to receive Jaiwa's messages. Whenever I begin to feel that I can't get everything done, and begin to pressure myself, I go into the temple. In any tense moment I pause and enter my temple to bring in the higher vibration.*

When I am alone in the timeless sense of my temple, my perspective about everything changes. All the people in my life are revealed to me in their true and loving selves. I see my own life as a wondrous journey of expanding consciousness. Every experience is revealed as important in teaching me about working, playing, loving, giving, and receiving from a profound gratitude for the source of life itself. Or I simply sense what is important to do now and what can be done next week. Once again I am back in harmony with my natural rhythm rather than feeling rushed or self-critical. I no longer am hesitant to be around lower or denser energies, although if I wish to be free of them I simply go to my temple, where they no longer exist.

TOOL OF LIGHT
CREATING YOUR TEMPLE OF LIGHT

T he following guided meditation will take you to the Temple of Light. Read these suggestions and do them in your mind as you read them. You might want to record the instructions and play them back while you listen in a relaxed state. I have provided tapes to take you through this and other meditations in the book.

Begin your journey by taking several deep breaths. As you breathe you can tighten and relax the muscles in your neck, shoulders, stomach, hips, thighs, and calves. Imagine that your muscles are perfectly tuned, just like the strings on a finely tuned Stradivarius.

Let each breath start deep in your stomach, expand your rib cage, and move up to fill your lungs. Feel the air fill your stomach as water fills a vase, from the bottom up. Pause briefly and exhale slowly, so gently that your breath would not blow out a match. After each breath pause briefly before inhaling again.

As you breathe deeply, transport yourself in your imagination to a beautiful meadow covered with brightly colored wildflowers. In this meadow, imagine a mountain stream and hear its bubbling sounds. You can decide to climb a mountain close by and find your temple among the trees at the very top of the mountain. Or you can simply imagine that the room around you is dissolving and you are calling to you the photons of light that create the form for your temple. Your temple is taking form at this moment. As you begin to image your temple you can feel its vibration and sense its luminous light.

Imagine that you are now standing at the entrance to your luminous Temple of Light. Is it a building? Or is it outdoors in a grove of trees? The more detail you can imagine, the more powerful its energy will be to assist you. Create the most beautiful place you can imagine. Is there a door? Notice its color and texture—even the details of carving on it. Look at the hinges that hold the door in place and the handle to open it. Reach out and grasp the handle firmly and slowly open the door.

If it has a physical structure, what does it look like inside?

How high are the ceilings? Does it have windows? Are they clear or stained glass? What are the walls made of? Are there rooms? How large are they? Are there crystals in your temple? What is the floor made of? Sit for a moment and fill in all the details of this beautiful space.

Does your temple have a garden? If so, identify some of the flowers and their fragrances. Do you hear any sounds of water or music or chimes around your temple? Add the sounds that please your esthetic senses.

Choose the area in your temple from which you will do your work with the light. You may want a chair or a soft cushion. What direction does it face? Add any other furnishings that you desire, such as a lovely desk, a large gemstone of pure colors, or whatever you sense will complete its beauty.

What colors are in and around your temple? Make each color more vivid and pure. Increase the light that is flowing into your temple. Do you see the photons of light as a soft glow or as a brighter light? Do you see short bursts of pinpoints of light? Or do you sense a blue or soft rose tint to the light here?

Add the sounds and the colors that are most harmonious to you. Add the final touches that will help you feel joyful or more loving.

Imagine that you are surrounded with the energy of many high beings and that your soul is expanded outward and upward. Know that as you sit in your temple your own energies are being refined and the note of your soul is penetrating all of your energy systems.

Ask for an inner message about what is the single most important thing you could do this week to open and grow spiritually. If you have a problem in your life, ask for a new understanding of it that will allow you to move through it more easily. Ask if there is anything you can do to become even more connected with these higher energies as you move through the day.

When you decide to leave the temple, reach over and touch your right hand to your heart. Later, by this touch alone, you can return in an instant to your temple. This signal gives you immediate access to it.

Your temple is for your journey into greater light and understanding. Honor it as your sacred place of wisdom, truth, serenity, love, and joy.

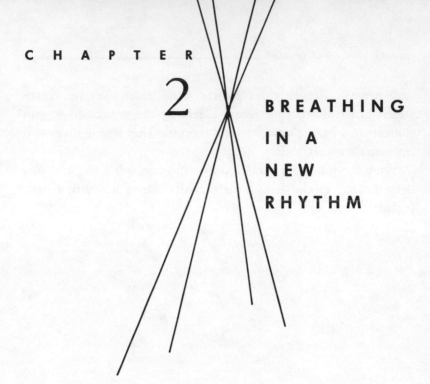

CHAPTER

2 BREATHING
IN A
NEW
RHYTHM

LAUNA **M**any years ago when I first be-
gan to study spiritual teachings from throughout the ages, I
would read about the importance of breathing, and for about
five minutes I would remember to breathe deeply. Even that
breathing was focused in my chest, cutting off the lower part of
my body. Then I would forget all about breathing again.

Later, during my graduate studies in neurophysiology, I was
impressed by the results of ongoing brain research showing that
the peak experiences of insight and mastery are characterized by
some very clear and easily recognizable patterns of brain activity
and that breathing rhythms are a critical factor in bringing
these patterns under conscious control. But it was not until
Jaiwa showed me how crucial breathing is to a more joyful and
aware quality of life that I realized my experiences of life mo-

ment to moment *are limited or expanded by my breathing.*

When I first began to verbalize and record my higher guidance and to ask all the questions I couldn't find the answers to, Jaiwa ignored my questions and began to teach me to breathe. As I channeled, it was made very clear to me that the more open my breathing was, the greater my potential would be for expanding my consciousness and making stronger, more powerful, and clearer connections with his energy field and with the God within.

JAIWA $\mathcal{A}$s you work with the light of your temple, you can greatly enhance your reception to its pure space by changing the rhythm of your breathing. New rhythms of breathing can facilitate your birth into greater light. The experiences you have are largely determined by the way you breathe. Although it may seem automatic and purely physical, how you breathe strongly influences your views and your values. It selects the windows through which you perceive the world and its meaning, both when you are with people and when you are in your temple.

When you are breathing shallowly, your brain does not get sufficient oxygen to do more than react to each situation in its accustomed fashion. You miss the opportunity to respond to people from your inner wisdom or from your heart. You even miss the higher truth of who you are. Many of your most serene and joyous experiences are made possible as you breathe more deeply and slowly.

When you breathe with deep natural breaths, you can be centered and focused. You can learn to breathe in ways that will bring extraordinary mental clarity. You can choose the realities you want to experience, such as abundance, adventure, good friendships, and loving relationships. You can sense the highest possibilities of your future filled with new understanding and delight.

Even as you imagine living in these realities, your breathing may deepen and slow down. As it does, the pulsing rhythm of your brain's signals changes too. There are many different wave patterns moving through your brain at the same time. These patterns are called brain waves.* They tend to be moving in different directions with different rhythms. As your breathing slows, your brain waves can move in a synchronized wave pattern. Deepen your breathing, and your perception changes. Thoughts become clear instead of scattered or confused. Optimistic feelings start to rise up. Your emotions tend to become calm and positive as breathing slows and the brain waves get longer.

Very shallow breathing propels the brain into fast frequencies and sets up a pressured feeling. It stimulates unconscious fears about survival (often the unconscious fears of others) and tends to become a repeating cycle. Prompt yourself with the words, "Remember to breathe, remember to breathe," the next time your breathing is too fast and shallow. Remember this one principle and you will be able to pull yourself out of fear or panic by simply changing the depth of your breathing.

Shallow breathing is contagious, and common to the world of competition. Because it keeps brain waves in rapid beta fre-

---

*LaUna: The human brain is composed of cells called neurons which transmit tiny electrochemical impulses. Each burst of electrochemical energy produces a corresponding electromagnetic field which can be measured. Regular patterns of electromagnetic activity are called brain waves. Brain waves are divided into groups by their characteristic frequencies measured in cycles per second, or hertz. So-called beta waves are in the range of 12 to 30 Hz, and are associated with intense mental activity. Alpha waves are 8 to 12 Hz, and appear during relaxation. Theta waves are between 4 and 8 Hz, and indicate light sleep, dreaming, or deep meditation. Delta waves, between 1 and 4 Hz, occur during deep sleep; they are rarely experienced by the conscious mind until a practice of meditation is well established.

quencies, shallow breathing causes feelings of pressure, of being somehow behind and needing to rush. In the reality dominated by these brain waves, much of life may be experienced as struggle. Grim overseriousness gets in the way of opportunities for happiness. A shallow breather's psychic immune system can be weakened and can leave her vulnerable to inner conflict and agitation. Even if someone has enough money to live comfortably for several months, shallow breathing can produce the experience of "not enough." People who live predominantly in beta states can use this energy to motivate themselves to find a better way. All they need to begin is a taste of their increased creativity and efficiency when their brain waves are synchronized by deep breathing.

You can learn to synchronize your brain waves and to change their frequency in order to connect with deeper dimensions of your inner wisdom. Slow brain waves consciously created by your breathing reveal an inner strength and stability and also a sense of joyous delight. Your power to fully love your life can be released with new rhythms of breathing as you work in your temple. You can find ways to make a real difference in the world.

If you find yourself caught in scattered thinking, you can change your brain waves to the slower alpha waves by simply deepening your breathing and feel an immediate release of tension. These brain waves help you think clearly because your mind slows down enough to focus on one thing at a time instead of jumping from one thought to another. Your thoughts are fluid and you are more creative.

Feelings of loneliness decrease and a sense of forgiveness for past mistakes offers an inner peace. Your sense of purpose becomes stronger, bringing a deeper understanding of why you are here at this time on this planet. Thus, a delight in simply being alive may begin in this state of consciousness.

If you continue to slow and deepen your breathing, you

can move into a deeper state of consciousness. Scientists recognize this state of consciousness by the brain waves called theta brain waves. With deep, slow theta breathing comes a sense of deep peace, often a feeling of ecstasy. You feel more loving, more accepting, more peaceful. You understand concepts that would seem like empty words with shallow breathing. At first it may seem unnatural to feel so serene and at peace. Human society is geared to fast frequencies and their constant movement in scattered directions. But the other world of reality, greater peace, and loving wisdom that exists in your temple is reached more easily by slowing and deepening your breathing. This state of consciousness will open for a larger portion of humanity as more people establish these new breathing patterns that give a direct access to the Higher Self.

Part of your regular nighttime sleep cycle takes you into a theta state. It is a state of serenity in which your body, emotions, and mind are at peace. The rhythm of theta brain waves allows your consciousness to slip out of the body and into other realities. This state comes in each night just before sleep, offering a window to solutions for problems. In this state you can go into the luminous light of your temple and experience a sense of yourself as a larger self without boundaries of time and space.

The slowest brain waves are found in delta and are usually formed only in deep sleep, though not always. We have watched some of you heal others from these delta brain waves. As soon as your healing is complete, your brain waves return to a normal alert state. Some of you who have been meditating a long time often display these very slow brain wave patterns in your meditations as you go into a higher consciousness.

Look for solutions to problems and conflicts in the brain wave state just slower than the one in which they were created. The solution may be obvious immediately, or it may come later and

seem like something you have always known but had temporarily forgotten. These answers don't always come in words;
they may come in a wave of positive feelings such as appreciation or delight.

Feelings of love, tranquility, and understanding signal that
your brain waves are moving closer to being in phase, and that
the left and right brains are becoming synchronized with the
vibration of your Higher Self. Even if you don't hear or feel
anything unusual, watch for the surrender of your mind to
serenity or the clarity of an inspiration or a sense of being fully
present. If you slow your breathing rhythm frequently enough,
there will finally come a switch in consciousness, and a deeper
breathing pattern will establish itself that no longer needs your
conscious attention. When you are meditating, for example,
you may notice that your breathing may seem to stop, but in
reality it is so expansive and slow, with natural rhythmic pauses
between each breath, that it is barely noticeable. You may only
be breathing three or four times a minute as your meditation
deepens. Yet your breathing won't be artificial or forced, but
natural and easy.

To open more fully to the energies of your temple, breathe
very deeply and slowly and each step will be revealed as you
master one and ask for more. Ask for what you want—a creative
approach to your highest vision, a greater stability to love
yourself, the clarity to understand the meaning of your life.
When your brain is fully nourished with oxygen, you can tap
into *how* to breathe to move into the coded wisdom of the
Higher Self. This knowledge is safely stored in your being and
is waiting to be activated.

You can stop whatever you are doing, sit down, and breathe
deeply for a few minutes, as you imagine vividly how it would
feel to be in a serene and joyful state. Get a sense of how you
would know if you were in this state. Breathe deeply until you
feel the touch of a greater love or understanding. Often that's all

it takes to start a gentle, nourishing sense of self moving through your body.

LAUNA In the *Bridge of Light* seminars we begin by experimenting with different rhythms of breathing and their effect on imagery. Some people have had powerful experiences in opening to new understanding in a problem situation.

In one session, Dan thought of his boss and felt his usual anxiety followed by a feeling of resentment. His chest felt too tight and restricted to breathe deeply for a moment. He deliberately deepened his breathing and entered his temple. Continuing to breathe very slowly and deeply, he felt calm again and imagined himself sailing across a nearby lake (it didn't matter that in real life he had no idea how to sail). Dan felt a wave of good feeling as the warm breeze ruffled his hair. From there, something wiser seemed to take over his fantasy. Dan "saw" his boss on another sailboat in the distance, struggling to keep it upright in high waves, fearful that he would take on too much water and sink. He saw the terrible insecurity and pain that his boss was suffering. At first Dan was happy to see his boss suffer, but as the other sailboat drew closer, he could see the agony on his face. He found himself reaching out to offer help as the boats drew closer together. Dan began to feel a real connection with his boss and imagined himself speaking freely and truthfully to him, acknowledging his own hurt. In his imagined reality they became good friends for the first time.

This visual exercise could have ended there, but to his amazement, the next day at work Dan discovered that there was a new connection with his boss. The boss came into his office, sat down, and talked over some touchy office problems with Dan, *as if he were talking to a good friend. There was no doubt in Dan's mind that his imagined meeting had happened only in his imagination, yet in the real world his boss was acting as if the connection had actually happened to both of them.*

None of us yet knows how profoundly new breathing rhythms can change our experiences. This man doesn't know how his exercise in breathing could have changed his relationship to his boss. He just knows that a strained and tense relationship has changed to an open and accepting one that is now warm and friendly—a change for which he is very grateful.

JAIWA Your rhythm of breathing is important because it is a key to activating brain cells and aligning them with the frequency of your temple. The ancients were correct: Meditation is the breath. Become the breath itself and memories of yourself as a soul will open once more. Becoming the breath feels to the personality like becoming nothing, but it is an opportunity to experience yourself as a soul of perfect beauty in the pure clear space of your temple.

TOOL OF LIGHT
CREATING A HIGHER ALIGNMENT
WITH YOUR TEMPLE

As you decide to enter the sacred energy of your temple, choose a symbol that reminds you to *breathe deeply and easily.* Some people choose a large, brightly colored balloon and see it being filled as they inhale and relaxed as they exhale. Choose any symbol that works for you. Begin to notice your breath. Count to seven as you inhale, pause one count, exhale to a count of seven, and pause one count. If a count of five to inhale, one to pause, and five to exhale is more comfortable, use that and then step into the entrance of your temple.

Take a deep breath, hold it, and let it go. Do it again. Feel the energy dance around in your forehead, then let it dance all through your brain, to the top and back of the brain. Keep breathing deeply. Bring the next breath into the lower part of your brain where it joins your spinal cord. Feel the energy there. Do it again. Draw the next breath into your heart. Feel the energy dance around your heart, and exhale. Breathe in again and exhale, this time through the top of your head. Continue these breaths through the top of your head for several minutes and then relax and breathe naturally. Practice each morning, and at any other break during the day. This way of breathing is preparing you for an adventure with light that can transform your life.

You can also visualize your breath coming through your feet, up through your spinal column, into your head. Let the breath create a sense of space around each cell in your body. For higher creativity or a clearer mind, breathe slowly and deeply, until you experience the powerful healing effect in your temple. Healing and rebalancing energies are always available to you in the higher frequency of your temple—and they are only a few breaths away.

3

RECEIVING TELEPATHIC IMPRESSIONS FROM THE GUIDES AND MASTERS

JAIWA Your personal guide and higher forces of the universe have also prepared a special room in your temple for receiving and sending information that is beyond your ordinary reach. This room is filled with pure light. It is located above the main room of your temple, approached by a graceful winding staircase. It is open to the natural breezes of the fresh mountain air and warmed by the sun. Close your eyes and see if your telepathic receiving room has clear and amethyst crystal panels in the walls and ceiling. You may want to build crystals into the room so they can amplify the reception of impressions and messages from greater sources of light. The beings of light and love who are watching over humanity's evolution can contact you in this room as well as your own guide. They can impress your mind with what you need to expand and grow spiritually and to be more effective in your work.

This room has broadcasting and receiving facilities for the astral, mental, and spiritual planes. The acoustics are perfect. You can set the dials for receiving or for sending messages of peace, freedom, hope, joy, and understanding. Here, you will find a natural and effortless connection with higher guidance whenever you need it. The crystalline formations in the room are set to resonate with the crystalline structures of your own body so that these impressions are clearly received and translated into ideas, thoughts, or words. You may feel your own body seeming to be electrified, your feet and hands tingling when you are sitting here.

When your intention to help humanity is clear, you will find your telepathic receiving room charged with a tremendous energy of light. You may feel embraced by a dimension of love that seems to permeate every cell in your body. In the energy field of the high guides who have mastered earth's lessons you are lifted into the greater awareness of the true nature of your essence and awakened to the grand benefits and rewards of a life on this planet.

Each time you go into this room, your guide amplifies the light and heightens your intuitive receiving. Training your intuitive reception takes daily practice, like playing the piano, but even when you are not aware of receiving knowledge or inspiration, much that we guides are sending is coming to you as intuitive ideas. We see you responding and we rejoice. We never withhold, although if we see that you are overloaded with new ideas, we slow them until you are able to handle the last surge.

You may receive impressions in the form of an inner knowing or deeper understanding of a higher truth rather than words. Even if your brain does not immediately translate the messages that are being received, they are impressed in your higher mind in this room. Over the next few days they will become clear to you. Nearly always you will perceive them as common sense, something that you suddenly see now which you somehow missed seeing before. You may suddenly think of calling an associate or friend and later discover that this person has the knowledge you were seeking. We often send people to assist you. Such meetings only seem like coincidences.

You will not always know the origin of the impressions received in this room. There are many dimensions of beings or intelligences who are both within and without your planetary system. Among them is a group of masters who are working specifically with the human race on this planet. They do not interfere with anyone's free will, because absolute free will is part of the purpose of this planet's evolutionary system. But when you turn to your Higher Self or God within, you put yourself into the stream of lighted energy created by the masters and the disciples who work with them from cosmic dimensions. It is on this column of light that their broadcasts are received.

The way we guides contact you (even our very existence) may seem puzzling, since we do not have a physical body or a physical voice. We are not more "spiritual" than you (although your languages lack definitive terms to discriminate our differences). All of us are simply in a position to offer assistance because we have unique Tools of Light, long experience with your planet, and a deep understanding of the laws and principles of the earth planet.

None of the guides appear in a physical form except in very rare and extreme circumstances. They come to you through the pure energy of a channel tuned to their frequency. Your stillness, openness, desire to understand more, and attunement to the light are what attracts these contacts to you. Above all, you attract assistance by your willingness to make a difference, not through personal ambition, but through perceiving some part of a larger plan for this planet and seeing where your own abilities and experience fit into that plan so that you can participate in it. Each master works with some part of a grand design for this planet to become one in which great love and wisdom are the natural mode of expression.

You can tune to some part of this plan from your crystal receiving room in your temple. Sometimes your personal ambitions may seem to coincide with this plan. At other times you will see how to expand or alter them so that they will be energized by the forces of light. Your desire to make a difference through serving in some way opens you to the line of lighted energy that goes through your own guide. The senior members (called masters) in this hierarchy can directly contact an individual who has offered his or her time and energy and who has precisely the experience and expertise needed for a specific project, but this kind of contact is rarely necessary. Using a wise economy of time and energy, they relay messages to your own guides, who then pass them on to you. Your guide may already be working closely with this group of planetary servers.

The guides are here to help you create a finer alignment to receive these messages as close as possible to their original meanings. We can focus light on you in this room and you may see creative possibilities for your life that had been out of your range of vision. There will be times when you are sitting in this room and the reception will be as clear as if you had received it from someone sitting directly in front of you. Your guide can contact you with direct telepathic impressions when he sees a need that you can fill, such as an open door for your work to get out, an important connection you can make, someone who needs your assistance, or a group you can work with.

Your own soul has a mechanism for control of too much coming in too fast. You may suddenly feel fatigued or want to stop thinking or meditating and simply go for a walk. Honor these urges and allow time to reflect on all that is flowing into your mind now. If too many ideas come in at once, they cannot all be acted upon without causing mental or emotional over-load. That is the problem with using artificial means to open the doors of perception: they may be opened too fast, and the result can be this kind of overload and subsequent feeling of exhaustion.

The messages that have influenced you the most may have seemed to come from yourself. They gave you hope when you felt hopeless, inspired you when you needed it, offered you new choices, or embraced you with love when you were isolated from loving friends. These messages originated from your own guide. By the time your conscious mind receives the message, it seems like you. This is what happens: we guides send messages as thought waves on currents of energy that are identified by their force of pure nonattached love. Your Higher Self picks them up and proceeds to step them down to your mind. As the align-ment between your higher mind and your brain is refined, the message goes to your conscious mind immediately. You receive it either from the left (logical) side of your brain in words or from your right brain in symbols and pictures.

Before these stepping-down processes and translations have taken place, you have already responded to the contact. When your spiritual body is stimulated by contact from a higher source, your personality is also stimulated. Your physical body is charged with great energy, your emotions are filled with an expansive sense of joy for no reason, your mind is crystal clear and organized. At these times you may be tempted to get busy in the mundane world, cleaning out closets or doing other ordinary chores, instead of quietly sitting in your temple to receive the wisdom and understanding that is poised to come into your conscious mind. When you feel such a charge of clear energy, go to your telepathic receiving room in your temple *before* you begin the day. You will find that your energy will be far more focused and effective.

The challenge that results from a stimulation by a high guide is that any personal ambitions for power or control which may lie under the surface of your awareness can also be stimulated. It is important for you, under the guidance of your Higher Self, to be in control, rather than allowing old ambitions to control you. We will show you many techniques for handling the sides of your personality that may be caught in the mass thought form of misusing power. You want to be able to count on every side of your personality to use its energy to cooperate with your *true* purpose.

As you practice receiving impressions from higher sources, you will want to be aware of how easily illusory reflections of the higher world can be confused with true contacts with the guides. These illusions can be quite lovely, but they do not have any real substance or carry the power of light or transformation in them. The way to break through the astral fogs that distort the higher truth is to release any ego-based desire to be contacted. An intense desire can actually block your guide's ability to reach you. When you place yourself in the service of humanity and focus on learning what you can do to help, you start clearing all barriers that could prevent a clear and pure connection.

LAUNA *Often, we receive an impression to take a certain action when we least expect it. The challenge we face is to listen, to discern the source, and, if we deem it to be coming from a wiser part of ourselves or from our guide, to honor the information. After completing this chapter, I was preparing to leave my office/temple, which is across the deck from my home, when I had a distinct impression to lock the door. "But I never lock the door. I'll only be gone a couple of hours," I argued with myself, "and anyway I have no idea where the key is." This dialogue went on for a few minutes while I* resisted honoring this information because the action seemed unnecessary. I decided to take my chances on a possible burglary because burglaries never happen here. At the split second I pulled the door closed, a piercing alarm began to ring—almost as if my door had triggered it. The alarm signaled that the house next door was being burglarized. No doubt the burglars would have immediately moved to my house and picked up my computer had they not been interrupted. This would have been a terrific loss to me—my entire manuscript was on the hard disk in the computer. I meekly opened the door and set the lock with a grateful heart for the timely warning, and made an inner promise to take the time to examine and honor all such impressions in the future—even though there might seem to be no apparent reason to do so.

EXERCISE
RECEIVING FROM HIGHER
SOURCES OF LIGHT

To make contact with or receive more clearly from your guides, first prepare your physical room to facilitate this reception. Set up the room to be as beautiful as possible. Put away all clutter. Light candles, bring in fragrant fresh flowers or incense, add beautiful pictures of nature or other symbols of spiritual grace. Fill the room with the sound of soft music, chimes, temple bells, or other nature sounds such as birds singing or ocean waves.

Sit in a comfortable position with your back supported and close your eyes. Mentally transport yourself to your crystal-domed telepathic receiving room in your Temple of Light as you begin to change the rhythm of your breathing. As you breathe deeply and slowly roll your neck, tighten and release your shoulders three or four times until you feel your body release all tension.

Offer your mind and your heart to the service of others. Feel your heart open with compassion.

Open to a peaceful, receptive mode without any expectation or specific problem in mind.

Imagine that there is a column of light coming from above and going straight through your body, straightening your spine, your head, and your neck, so that they are in perfect alignment.

Continue to breathe deeply and to be in a state of relaxed joy. Imagine that the luminous light in this room is changing to a warm, liquid light and gradually spreading throughout your body.

After no more than twenty or thirty minutes of sitting in this mode of reception, begin to write or record the ideas that you are receiving. Sometimes a part of you will say that you didn't receive anything, but by writing something on a page or speaking some phrase into the tape recorder, you may be able to tap into the impressions received and put them into words. Or simply record descriptions of your state of consciousness, such as, "I feel at peace, calm, serene, joyful, transcendent, at one, in harmony with the universe." Every acknowledgment that you can offer in writing strengthens the column of light that brings your brain into alignment with your higher mind and your higher mind into alignment with your soul and with your guide.

You can sit in your telepathic receiving room every day if you wish, or once a week. A regular time and place are helpful to increase your clear reception. Trust your intuition and your inner wisdom.

4

SENDING TELEPATHIC MESSAGES TO OTHERS FROM YOUR TEMPLE

LAUNA We can't always express to people what we really feel or think. Misunderstandings arise and we don't know how to heal them. Sometimes we need to communicate with people who are not open to us, who have such different beliefs that we can't get through to them. Other people we want to reach may live in another town or country, unavailable by phone or letter. Telepathy bypasses people's normal defenses and resistances and connects us to each other's essence and love. It can help us to communicate higher messages of harmony and love to our husbands, wives, friends, children, bosses, and even to people we will never meet personally.

JAIWA You can consciously send powerful broadcasts without physical contact.

Your broadcasts go out on three vibratory levels: from the emotional or astral center, from the mind, and from the soul. You can send messages that carry healing and inspirational energies on any of these levels. They are received by anyone who has a matching open channel of reception, much like a short-wave radio receiver.

The first and most frequently used telepathic energies are in the emotional or astral plane. Did you ever find yourself feeling happy around another person for no special reason? You were reflecting his or her basic emotional tone. People frequently send and receive on this plane, and its energy is quick to filter through to other people. If a friend needs cheering and you sense his need, it is natural to respond and send him an energy of good will and encouragement. He does not have to direct his request to you. You can pick it up telepathically and send what is needed.

Before you plan to consciously send assistance to someone, you will want to recognize which plane he or she is primarily functioning on and broadcast to him or her from that dimension so that the channels will be compatible and your message can be received with accuracy. Some people work almost entirely from their mental selves and would not respond to a message sent by way of an astral stream of energy.

You can broadcast on powerful streams of mental energy.

The second plane for telepathic sending is the mental plane. As you master the ability to hold your mind in the light, free of any emotion, you are ready to send pure mental messages to others. You can broadcast thoughts to people you know and to groups worldwide.

The precise frequency of your mental broadcast depends on the tone or note of your own thoughts. They go on the beams that can carry them most efficiently. When you broadcast an idea, the other person or group can receive it the moment their own thoughts slow and they become receptive. This often happens during the night or just before sleep. They won't know from whom it came, but will simply receive what is needed as an inspiration or idea. Some people will receive your thoughts with ease and respond immediately. You may have noticed this in routine thoughts. You think of calling someone on the telephone to deliver a message and before you dial the number the person has called you.

The telepathic joining of higher minds makes true progress on the physical plane possible. Everything that is known by humanity from any age is stored on the mental planes and can be tapped into by anyone who can consciously perceive the messages at that high frequency. The finest ideas floating in the higher mental planes are there for anyone to tap into. You have probably drawn from this pool many times and benefited from the vast knowledge which exists there. Those working in the same field with you (from the past or the present in earth time) contribute knowledge which adds to the effectiveness of your work as you absorb these ideas. Your highest ideals, your inspirations, and your positive visions can also add to this pool of knowledge.

Broadcasting soul to soul heals all imbalances.

The third kind of broadcast involves a soul-to-soul communication. These broadcasts always carry healing power. The energy that goes out from your soul to the soul of another is pure and clear, without any distortion from emotions. It comes from a very deep place within your being and may be in the form of symbols (words, pictures, objects) or simply a point of light.

You can broadcast on more than one channel. You may send a message from the soul channel and the mental channel. Before you started reading this book, for example, you may have received some parts of it telepathically. As you recognize ideas you have already received, you may wonder where the knowledge came from. This is an example of a soul-to-soul broadcast. It may also be true of many other books you read that are focusing on the spiritual planes. The more people who are tuning to the line of lighted energy of soul broadcasts, the more easily others receive. Even if you are not writing a book on paper, you may be writing it on other planes as you receive and then send from soul levels with the intent to serve all who can be benefited. When enough people are focusing light toward humanity with the desire to help, a great opening can take place and motivate many people to take another step toward the source of light.

LAUNA H*ere are several examples of telepathic sending on mental and spiritual channels in which the results were immediate and unmistakable. They went out on a high frequency and in each case were sent with no selfish purpose but were motivated from compassion and love.*

Margaret, a 41-year-old woman from Boston, came to Jaiwa for help with her relationship with her husband. They had been going through chronic tension as a couple, and were at a standstill when they finally discussed their problems. She had a long list of changes she wanted him to make, but he wasn't changing anything. Jaiwa led her through a telepathic soul essence broadcast to her husband. From her temple she felt very loving and accepting of him. She sent this dimension of love to him with the message, "I accept you and love you exactly as you are now." From her soul level this was true.

To Margaret's amazement, her husband responded within twenty-four hours by shortening his long work hours so that he could spend more time with her. Soon he began to reach out to her with affectionate hugs in place of the familiar, silent distancing. Next, he began to find ways to help at home. Suddenly Margaret realized that he was doing everything she had wanted since receiving her essence message of love.

As soon as he received her loving, accepting message, he became a receptive and giving partner. His resistance had been escalated to balance her constant push for him to change. The new message made of soul light illuminated her mind as well; she saw how irritating her pressure must have seemed to him. Instead of long reasoning discussions, they began to spend their time together from a sense of appreciation. In this atmosphere of gentle acceptance and recognition of each other's nobility, they could discuss their individual needs from each other's standpoints.

These broadcasts work with babies as well as adults. Rebecca, my 15-month-old goddaughter, was extremely unhappy with her new babysitter. The other three toddlers who stayed with this sitter seemed contented, but Rebecca cried every time her mother left her and was often crying when her mother came to pick her up. Something was clearly wrong; the situation had been going on for three weeks.

Her mother and I decided that if she wasn't happy by the end of the week, she should not have to return. The mother agreed to sit down with Rebecca and send a message through the soul's stream of energy. Although the mother admitted feeling a little silly, she sat Rebecca down and sent this message to her. She used words to help herself feel more comfortable, explaining that she wanted her to be happy, and if she couldn't manage to like the sitter and be happy there she would not have to go back after Friday. That was all—a straight message of love and compassion from the heart of the mother to the heart of her daughter.

The next morning Rebecca seemed less reluctant than usual on the ride to the babysitter's house. When it came time for the mother to leave her usually reluctant child, Rebecca walked over to the sitter and threw her tiny arms around her. Both the sitter and the mother were amazed. Rebecca then settled down to play with the other children. Every day after that she went into her play school, calmly greeted her sitter, and began to play with the other children.

I enjoy showing mothers of babies and young children how to send a silent message to their children to remind them that they are beings of light and love. I often send these messages in the grocery store when a crying child passes me. The response is usually dramatic no matter how great the physical distance between us. The children's fretfulness immediately changes to serenity as they receive this awareness. I believe it reaches them through the soul level because even babies are profoundly affected. Sometimes the change of mood from fretting to peacefulness is so sudden that it surprises me.

An even more dramatic example happened a few years ago, when a group of us, including two of my sons, Donald and Ray, went white water rafting with a tour on the challenging King's River of southern California. We went just for the adventure and fun of it. But the snows had melted late and the river was running at flood stage. In less than ten minutes on the river we were in serious trouble. Our raft was overturned by fifteen-foot waves and all of us were swimming for our lives in the icy water as the current pulled us under again and again. Our guide was knocked unconscious by the force of the wave. Although the immediate threat was drowning, we each knew that we had about twelve minutes to get out of the icy water before we succumbed to hypothermia and the consequent paralysis of our muscles. For one brief moment I saw my good friend John gulping helplessly as he choked, and then I was whisked away on the next wave.

Minutes later I was picked up by our group's emergency oar boat ahead, but none of the others appeared. We were carried so swiftly in the rushing water that we were already a mile further downstream. As soon as we could stop bailing and get in quiet water, I realized that I was absolutely helpless to do anything to help save my friends. I could sense that John was in a life-and-death struggle. Then I remembered to go into my temple, get very still, and broadcast from the soul a clear message for help from the higher guides. Next, I sat quietly in the oar boat, waiting to hear. An hour passed and no word. Suddenly, I received a very terse but clear message, "John is safe," and I knew without a doubt, even though there was no visible sign of hope, that he was safe.

In another half hour the other raft from our expedition rounded the corner. John, Donald, and Ray were waving wildly from the front of the loaded boat. The rafting guide had some-how managed to get her raft to a tiny island in the middle of the high waves. John told us how he had almost given up. Nearly paralyzed by hypothermia and unable to see anything without his glasses, he was pummeled by the rocks as he was swept downstream. Finally he found some rocks to cling to in shallow water, but found the current too swift to try to get on the tiny island ahead. Donald and Ray waded out and formed a human chain to pull him onto the sand with the others. He had reached the tiny island of safety at the precise time that the message was sent to me.

I was shown later that beings from the inner planes received my signal for help and beamed a higher frequency of awareness to John and then telepathically sent the message to me that he was safe. This kind of communication and power to help is *always available to us when we can remember to calmly tune to the higher frequencies and, even if only for a moment, to be free of emotional reactions.*

EXERCISE
SENDING TELEPATHIC BROADCASTS ON THE MENTAL AND SOUL PLANES

The telepathic sending room is now ready for your presence. Recall the circular staircase, the domed roof, and the walls of amethyst panels before you enter your temple. You can tune the dials to soul, mental, or astral frequencies. Here, you can set the dials for sending a message to any individual you wish, to a group, such as the children of the world, or to all of humanity.

Take several very deep slow breaths as you prepare to go to your temple. You may find that walking across a beautiful meadow and up to the mountaintop where your temple is located assists you to prepare to enter it. As you open the door with your name on it and step into the entrance, sit in the center and clear your own energy field as you absorb the light of your temple.

Next, walk up the narrow winding staircase to your crystal-domed telepathic sending and receiving room. Take a few minutes to examine the instruments here.

Think of the person or group you wish to send a message to until you have a sense of their faces or their voices. If you are thinking of a large group, such as all the children of the world, or the people of your town, imagine the light from your Higher Self sending simultaneous rays of light to the heart of each one. Your sending capacity is expanded by your active imagination.

Your message may be very brief:

"Live fully and in peace."

"Love your life."

"Be joyful."

"You are free to live from the authority of your own soul."

Deliver your message, feeling the power of each word in it as you do. See people responding to your message and then release the connection in the same way that you hang up the telephone when you are through speaking.

S E C T I O N II

BRIDGE

OF

LIGHT

This section presents you with a very powerful Tool of Light to bring great joy, love, and wisdom to your life. You will begin to construct a Bridge of Light, learning step-by-step how to spin this bridge from the heart center of your being to the center of each spiritual quality. Next, you will construct a bridge to the spiritual self of someone you know or to a group you wish to help. In the following three chapters you will spin a Bridge of Light to three key qualities of the soul: love, joy, and courage. The Bridge of Light is a pathway to integrate the power and beauty of every soul quality into your everyday responses—from wisdom and truth to humor and delight.

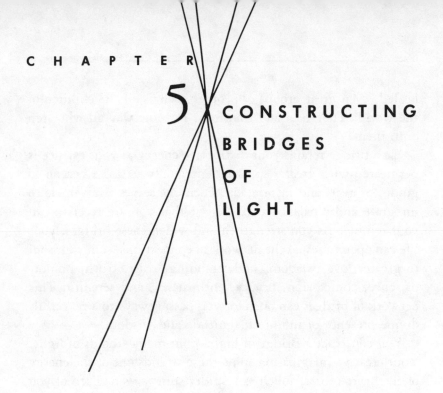

CHAPTER

5 CONSTRUCTING

BRIDGES

OF

LIGHT

JAIWA Now that you have prepared a
sacred place from which to expand your consciousness, you
are ready to bring the greater light of spiritual energy into all
of your relationships and your work. You are ready to learn
how to construct a Bridge of Light. You will be creating
these magnificent bridges throughout the book to gain new
understanding and knowledge, to manifest your true purpose,
and to bring into your life all the joy and fulfillment that the
spiritual energies hold for you once you know how to use
them.

Bridges of Light can create profound and lasting changes in
every aspect of your life. You can use them to create more loving
relationships. They instantly connect you to anyone anywhere in
the world. You can bring anyone onto your bridges to be

healed, even great groups of people, such as all the children of the world. They heal and transform in some way all who step onto them.

Each bridge retains your distinctive energy as your essence is permeated with greater spiritual energy. It acts as a beacon to guide, protect, and inspire you. Each one serves as a vehicle to integrate and rebalance all the light that you are receiving in your temple. As you strengthen and widen these bridges, your life can open to reveal the network of connections from your soul to greater love, wisdom, understanding, trust, truth, humor, patience, compassion, beauty, enthusiasm, and serenity. This network of bridges can open for you passageways to a powerful, divine presence of infinite magnitude and wisdom.

You construct a Bridge of Light from many strands of light. Your creative imagination spins these strands out of the energy of the heart center, much as a spider spins a web. Each of you focuses lines of lighted energy in a pattern that is your own. Anywhere you have a deep desire for greater understanding, healing, or effectiveness is an appropriate place to establish a Bridge of Light.

Each Bridge of Light you build can focus light on and dissolve another layer of confusion that has prevented you from realizing your own divinity. Until now, the experience of one's innate divinity has been mostly unavailable except through years of working with a spiritual master. It was not purposely withheld from a sincere seeker, but could only rarely be reached from the vibration that humanity lived in. Only a few people in each generation who were sincerely attempting to make the jump to a higher vibration were able to connect with the larger world of their divinity powerfully enough to be released from the illusions of life on this planet. As humanity is rapidly expanding its awareness, these altered and high states of consciousness are now opening to each person to experience directly.

The guided meditation at the end of the chapter shows you how to construct a Bridge of Light.

A Bridge of Light brings the energy of a higher soul quality into your life.

The first thing you want to do with your Bridge of Light is to connect with the higher qualities of your soul, such as compassion, wisdom, love, truth, trust, aliveness, enthusiasm, joy, and humor. These higher qualities will change the way you see yourself, your friends and your work. Connecting with these qualities gives you the inner strength and wisdom to fully recognize what you really want. Bridges of Light are the key to bringing you everything that you want—loving relationships, success, peace of mind.

As you spin Bridges of Light from yourself to different facets of the light, such as humor, harmony and joy, be prepared to experience lighter sides of your being. Each successive state of awareness may still seem like it is just you, but it is a "you" who is wiser, more serene and compassionate than the "you" of the day before. It includes the previous "you" and expands it at the same time. As you progress, it may be hard to realize how much has become easy that used to be a struggle, or how much more flexibility you have developed in thinking, or even how much lighter and happier you feel.

Build a Bridge of Light to another person and change your relationships.

You can send a Bridge of Light from your heart to the heart of a friend through the quality of love. Love in all of its forms—compassion, trust, truth, honesty—will transform any relationship even if the other person isn't involved in this way of working. Every connection you make to someone using a

Bridge of Light is real on its own plane of existence. Imagine that it looks exactly like a bridge between you and the other person, extending from your heart to her heart, so real that you can walk across it. It cannot be diminished by distance or outside interferences. You are establishing a communication which is beyond the physical world, even beyond language, but which can affect the mental, emotional, and physical energies in extraordinarily positive ways. Your connection embraces your friend's whole being and allows her an opening to embrace your own whole being.

When you want to send a loving message to a loved one or friend, you can spin a Bridge of Light to the quality of love and absorb its energy. After you sense its warm, tingling, peaceful vibration permeating each cell in your body, you can spin another bridge to the heart of a friend. From your temple you can walk out on your bridge to meet your friend in the middle. You won't need to know what he needs. Simply trust that the quality of love will be the *right* one to empower and enrich his life and change your relationship for the better.

You can spin bridges to your children and bring new levels of courage, delight, humor, and confidence to their lives both at home and at school. They are very receptive to these Bridges of Light and to any work done on these higher planes of consciousness. Children easily learn to spin their own bridges and take delight in using them as tools to help each other and the "big people" as their sense of compassion and caring expands.

Your Bridge of Light cannot take away the free will of another. You are inviting a relationship of light. Your friend's soul or heart center filters the light you send through her own soul or heart energy. The result is that the people you have connected to from your bridge are freer to express themselves with love and wisdom, not only to you, but to all the people in their lives. Almost everyone is able to accept a loving connection offered in this way.

One session of a Bridge of Light connection can take the hunger out of the heart and the tension out of the body. Sometimes the light of the bridge hits you with a kind of electrical current, and there is a momentary dizziness or a feeling of interior spaciousness. This experience rejuvenates your spirit and your mind.

A Bridge of Light can reach anyone anywhere in the universe.

Once a bridge spans the distance from your temple to the person you choose, you have made a connection. These connections help bring your visions to you, one step at a time. For example, they can bring new structure to a relationship so that it will be more joyful and fulfilling to both people.

Bridges of Light encourage a loving understanding between people, even if they have different beliefs and goals.

As the energies of light are pouring into the planet, everything has to be adjusted to a higher level of harmony. Things that have been out of harmony demand attention. Even situations that used to feel fine may need to be adjusted to your new, finer vibration, just as one violin in an orchestra brought to a finer pitch is the inspiration for the other violins to be tuned up as well.

If struggle or conflict does come up, it is because every increase in light brings new challenges as it opens a larger vision of what is possible. You may be blaming yourself because you are still having conflicts in your relationships, even though you are trying to be loving. This greater light will challenge you to let go of old patterns of control, jealousy, possessiveness, or resentment. To let go of them they often have to come up as issues between you and your loved one so that you can heal them. A single bridge to the Higher Self or soul of another person can open up a channel of connecting that is loving and supportive. The more love you generate between yourself and another person, the more possible it is for past wounds to be healed.

When you want to connect from the heart with someone you know, or with a group whose work you feel aligned with, build a Bridge of Light to them. You can use your bridge to heal conflicts where there has been hurt, disagreement, or separation. It can remove the illusions of scarcity from a situation and reveal the underlying abundance. Feelings of scarcity of love, self-worth, time, energy, or money can change as the transforming energy of your bridge flows into your being.

You can use a Bridge of Light in every area of your life.

If you have a tight muscle or stiff neck, a Bridge of Light to wisdom can reveal the cause. Once you can sense what anxiety or fear has lodged in your body you can focus on the part that is in pain and break the hold of fear through your new knowledge. Energy is very useful once it is loosened from a fear pattern. Fluid and free energy nourishes your life.

You can build Bridges of Light to a job, a home, a trip, or a project you want. You can create your highest possible future by learning how to construct Bridges of Light. There is no limit to how many bridges you can construct. The more you build, the more stability of light you bring into your life. This creates an inner strength and a clear focus toward your most powerful life purpose. Each bridge can change an old way of thinking and acting. Living and serving to your highest potential is made possible as you penetrate every feeling, memory, or thought of the future with Bridges of Light.

When you go to bed at night, spin a Bridge of Light to a soul quality, such as wisdom, clarity, or joy. It will take you to a higher dimension in your dreams and continue its work of healing and enlightening as you sleep. When you awake, construct a Bridge of Light to the same quality, even before you put your feet to the floor. The whole tone and feeling of your day will be greatly enhanced.

At every point in your spiral of opening to more light, you can build new bridges—each one standing erect and powerful. As soon as you reach one dimension of the light and become familiar with it, another jump in consciousness opens beyond that—and another and another. Each one brings new challenges and responsibility as well as new opportunities to contribute to the planet through your life force.

LAUNA A *woman in one group I spoke to was in a state of deep sorrow because her path was so different from her husband's. He was a prominent surgeon and she was an artist. The intention and purpose behind their work seemed so far apart to her that she felt deep loneliness and isolation on her spiritual path. As she walked out on her Bridge of Light, which she had intended to spin to the quality of compassion, she discovered that her husband was approaching her from the other end. When they met in the middle, they embraced and wordlessly reconnected. She felt such a powerful love from him that a great weight dropped from her shoulders. She suddenly realized that although he did not speak in "spiritual" terms, he was as dedicated as she was to finding ways to add something valuable to people's well-being and happiness. As she described what had happened, her face softened to reveal a hidden beauty and youth,* and her voice dropped to a lower pitch and slowed as she spoke of someone she loved very deeply.

It is not only the changes that happen to the bridge builder that are profound; the receiver of light seems to change as dramatically, even though he or she does not consciously know about the meeting on the bridge. One 45-year-old woman from Houston who had suffered a deep split in her relationship with her sister for nine years decided to build a bridge composed of the light of pure understanding to her sister. When she walked out on the bridge and reached her sister, she realized that she accepted her just as she was and that all past misunderstandings were forgiven. Standing on her bridge, she told her sister this and held her for a moment in her arms. Within two weeks her sister called her and talked with the love and warmth that they had enjoyed before the split happened. It was as if the hurts had never happened at all. The bridge builder was stunned in disbelief. The separation between them had dissolved without the need for long discussions and explanations. In the higher dimension of light, healing can happen in an instant; love can be restored in a flash.

What happens if we spin Bridges of Light to each other, and form a network of lighted lines of energy between our Higher Selves on the higher planes before we attempt to communicate on the physical plane? Donna, a strong light worker, did just this. She constructed a Bridge of Light to a friend in another city, not for any special reason, just to connect soul-to-soul.

As she stood on her bridge her hands became warmer, her chest suddenly felt free and expanded, her body became very relaxed and at peace. No words were spoken as Donna and her friend met in the center and were engulfed by the great light on the bridge. Three days later the friend called to say she had suddenly been inspired with a wonderful plan for Donna's work. Out of loving compassion and under the inspiration of her guide, this friend then spent several days mapping details of the *plan to assist Donna. The inspiration proved to be a key point in Donna's success and actually was the turning point in her career.*

TOOL OF LIGHT
CONSTRUCTING A BRIDGE OF LIGHT

Y ou can spin a powerful Bridge of Light to the radiating energy of a soul quality that will enrich your life now. Perhaps you never thought of yourself as light and humorous, and would like to bring that quality to your life. Or you may want to have a clear sense of purpose, a connection with beauty, or a feeling of love or compassion. You may decide to bring more wisdom and understanding into your life. From your temple you can create a connection to any of these higher soul qualities through the power of your Bridge of Light.

Some of the major soul qualities which you may want to bring into your life are:

Wisdom	Oneness
Love	Acceptance
Truth	Patience
Trust	Perseverance
Courage	Higher organization
Joy	Vision of the future
Confidence	Peace
Humor	Enthusiasm
Beauty	Serenity
Harmony	Understanding
Heart connection	

Find a place where you won't be disturbed for about fifteen minutes. Sit in a comfortable chair and loosen any tight clothing. Begin by taking seven deep breaths, tightening and relaxing the muscles in your body, noticing the thoughts in your mind and the state of your emotions. Walk across a meadow covered with wildflowers and climb a mountain until you see your Temple of Light. If there is a door, look at your name on the door as you open it, and then stand in the entrance to the temple. Inhale deeply as you enter and sit in the center, allowing the shimmering light of your temple to penetrate the cells of your body and your mind. Breathe deeply until you feel very calm and relaxed. After a few moments of experiencing a tingling or peaceful sense of self, connect with one of the soul qualities that would most enrich your life now.

Imagine a great ball of light somewhere in the vast universe of higher consciousness which is the source of that quality—the place where it grows and expands. Using the quality of joy as an example, imagine a tremendously benevolent and powerful sphere of light which is the source of all joy, and picture it expanding with every breath. If the light seems too intense, use your imagination to soften it and give it a tint of blue or yellow, or add filters so that the light is comfortable.

Breathe into your heart several times and imagine that each breath is opening and expanding your heart center. Next, imagine that you are spinning strands of light from your heart center (located between your shoulders and a few inches away from your body) to the core energy of joy.

Focus completely on the strands of light as you spin them one by one, until they form a bridge. Add more strands until you feel the connection is getting solid and strong. Now open to receive the energy of joy as it flows to you across your Bridge of Light. Breathe deeply in order to draw this energy into your whole being. Notice the images that come to you, the thoughts or feelings of what joy is at its source.

Now anchor your bridge in the temple and walk across it to the very center of joy. Feel the difference there.

You may want to return to the center of joy many times.

Each time you return, the bridge will be noticeably stronger and wider. You will feel much more stable and sure of yourself as you walk across it. Or you may want to spin Bridges of Light to several different qualities in succession, such as clarity, humor, and compassion. Decide what qualities would so enrich your life at this time that you hardly dare dream of the difference they could make, and walk directly across your bridges to the core of each of them.

TOOL OF LIGHT
CONSTRUCTING A BRIDGE OF GOLDEN
LIGHT TO A PERSON

Select one significant relationship which is profoundly affecting your life now, even if the other person lives far away. Or you can choose someone whom you admire or appreciate and yet do not feel truly connected to. It can be someone you have never met or someone you have known for a long time.

The healing effect that this exercise has on your body can be as powerful as the effect it has on your spirit, mind, emotions. As you heal a relationship and strengthen the heart connection, you are also establishing a stronger connection to your Higher Self from some part of your personality that has felt alienated from it.

Close your eyes and breathe as you have practiced in Chapters 2 and 3. Be sure that your breath fills your stomach first, then your rib cage, then your lungs. As you exhale, imagine that any impurities in your energy field are being released at the same time. After you have done this for a few minutes, notice if your hands have become warmer and your breathing easier and more expanded than before.

After the rejuvenation of breathing deeply several times, bring the soul quality of love into your breath and imagine a glowing energy emanating from your heart center. Visualize strands of light that are permeated with the energy of love being spun from the substance of your heart center. See your life force propelling them as they begin to form a Bridge of Golden Light.

Send these strands of light to the heart center of your friend and see it take on a clearly recognizable glow as you imagine it. Keep adding strands until you have a solid Bridge of Light and are beginning to feel the heart connection with your friend. When you have a solid bridge prepared, anchor the bridge firmly to your temple and walk out on it. As you begin crossing the bridge, experience the grace and beauty that you have created. Your friend is very likely to meet you in the center of the bridge. When you meet, allow yourself to feel a deep acceptance of each other just as you both are right now. Honor the being of your friend and feel the united spirit of your heart connection and its powerful gift of love.

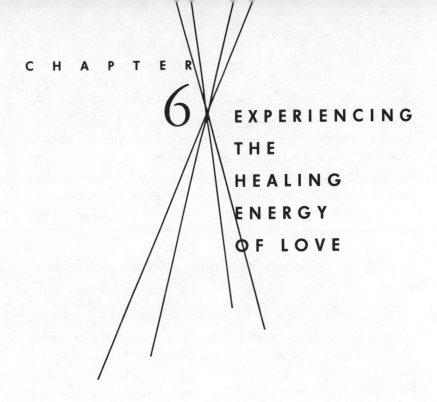

CHAPTER

6

EXPERIENCING
THE
HEALING
ENERGY
OF LOVE

JAIWA T he next three chapters offer you
the three major soul qualities you will need to integrate the
frequencies of light that are moving across the planet now. They
are love, joy, and courage. (Beliefs in spiritual growth only
through long suffering, misery, and self-depreciation are no
longer appropriate in these higher frequencies.) Few of you
received this training from conception and birth, but you can
now integrate these new patterns through the power of your
Bridges of Light. Your own children will then carry these new
patterns of courageously expanding into greater light through
love and joy as their natural inheritance.

Perhaps the most challenging of all the new patterns is that
of the soul quality of love. Many of you are asking why love is
such a challenge in your relationships and how you can experi-

ence love as a source of healing and joyful interaction with others in your life. Asking questions about love helps to open your heart's wisdom. Whatever you ask becomes the tool to draw forth the answer that already lies within you. The answer may come as an inspiration to express a new frequency of love with someone in your life. You may sense how valuable your love is to your friends and want to find new ways to act on the deep caring you feel.

Each of you is learning to express a higher dimension of love.

Love is the healing force of the universe. The mysterious interactions of the atoms and molecules in your body are a story of love. Their cooperation to form order and harmony are expressions of love. Everything that is growing and vitalized by life spirit is held in place by this vibrant, expanding, glowing life force.

Love is the essential nature of your being. Many of the dimensions of love could not be expressed in the dense energies of this planet until now. As you open to these finer frequencies in your sacred temple the essence energy of love will begin to flood into your life. You are expressing love at this moment with every breath. You can enhance and deepen your awareness of it by breathing deeply. In the same way, you can breathe in photons of love from a special place in your temple and receive deep levels of healing love. You actually begin to glow with a luminous light around your body when you open to the love in the universe.

When you are glowing with the radiance of love you heal the people that you are with.

You can construct a Bridge of Light to love from your temple, and experience it as if the sun were breaking through a very dense fog. Soon the air feels clear, the sky looks blue again, the clouds fluffy and white. This happens when you touch the shimmering, glowing, luminous essence of this invisible quality called love. When you are in this state of loving people, they naturally rise to a higher state when they are with you. Their expansiveness increases to match yours. They can make a similar connection to the force of love, because any negative thoughts in their field of energy are dismantled in the glow of your loving presence.

We see how enriched and powerful your life would be if you felt absolutely free to express the deep level of love that is sounding its note within you now. As we guides watch you, we see that you each have a different note, even a different hue. You express love from subtly different vibrational tones. That is why it is so interesting to observe you. Each person has a particular note and color through which his or her love is expressed.

Give love only when it feels joyful.

You may feel as if you give more love than you receive at times. When giving love takes effort and does not give you an expanded feeling, the people you are with have reached their limit of receiving. Their resistance is revealed when you feel it is effortful to talk or be loving with them. They are doing the best they can. No one wants to receive more love (or anything else) than he or she can give, because the scales are not balanced and disharmony results.

From our perspective, there is no way that you can give more love than you receive. You may not always receive from the people you give to, but the love that you give to others simultaneously goes into your own life—healing any regrets, guilt, or mistakes—one layer at a time. It flows into your mind and heals it, and into your emotions and heals them. It flows into your past and into your future. It flows all through your life. Love is a facet of the luminous light. This sounds mystical, but there is no scientific term to use because it is not visible to the human spectrum of sight. Its reality has not yet been proved in the laboratories, yet we know that you can send love to anyone in the world and they receive it instantly.

Before you are with others, you can first imagine them standing on a Bridge of Light that you have constructed to love. See this bridge shining with a luminous light as both of you inhale its healing essence into your minds and bodies. Later when you are with these people who are special to you, think of the essence of love that is within them. When you focus on that point of inner light radiating from their heart center, you are inviting a heart connection between you. Their response might not come in the words you expect or in the action you had pictured. You recognize that they have responded within and opened their heart because *you* feel more expanded. Does your heart feel more open? Do you feel lighter? Stronger? Wiser? If so, you know that the love stimulated by your love is reverberating back and forth between you. These people are very likely to feel happier, stronger, and more centered after being with you.

We guides see you sending love to others again and again. As the energy of love is sent, the souls of the receivers absorb it in a way that fits their vibrations. Soon, a strong feeling of new hope, a greater vision, or a surge of optimistic clarity will filter into their minds and emotions. They almost always experience this enriched awareness as their own, rather than coming from someone else. It will give them the freedom to put this loving energy where it best serves their purpose at this time. It may not change them in the way you expect, but the impact of the higher energy of love will assist them to see with greater clarity and openness. Send the quality of love from your temple with the desire for it to work for everyone's highest expression.

Your Temple has a place of healing love.

In this place all hurt and disappointment dissolves. You can absorb a new dimension of love here. Particles of electromagnetic radiance flow into this space. You may want to create a soft mat in the center of it to absorb the full power of these photons of love. If you need to heal or rejuvenate yourself you can lie on this mat and experience great love. You can also bring in anyone who requests your help and have him sit with you or lie directly on the mat while you spin a Bridge of Light to him from the quality of love. There is a special transparency in this healing space that will enable you to sense what is needed.

Each one of you can receive from the great energy source of love. As you absorb love on a regular basis, your own energy field gradually takes on its radiance. As it becomes more steady, your radiant field of energy can lift sadness, grief, or loss from another person without a word being spoken. Each person has the freedom to accept or reject it, but the invitation is there to experience the healing essence of love and to remember again who he or she really is.

In your place of healing love you may experience forgiveness for things that have long bothered you, or realize that what you have considered your greatest problems actually offer your greatest opportunities to expand. Your experiences in your temple may be very difficult to put into words, but the difference they make in your everyday life is the real test of their power. Allow yourself many sessions in this place for your heart to absorb the kind of nourishment that is simply not obtainable from other people.

TOOL OF LIGHT
THE HEALING PLACE OF LOVE

The following exercise is from a series of twelve audiotapes by Jaiwa called *Soulplay*. Each tape in the series focuses on amplifying a specific soul quality in your life. (For information, refer to Appendix.) You can use the ideas from these tapes and create your own personal series of Soulplay tapes, recording them to music or to the sound of waves. Listening to these tapes with headphones is a tranquilizing and powerful experience. The more you listen, the more solidly you can impress new patterns of love (or joy or wisdom or humor) on the unconscious and conscious sides of your mind.

Just reading this exercise slowly once will take you into the enriched state that love gives to you. Or if you wish you can practice it many times.

Take a moment to get very comfortable. Lie back with your eyes closed, loosen your clothes, and breathe deeply, easily. Let go of every thought about the day, every anxiety, every thought of being rushed, or busy, and allow yourself plenty of time to experience a very deep love from within your own being.

To deepen your connection to the quality of love, enter your Temple of Light in the main chamber and step into the space where the convergence of energies is most powerfully focused. Is it in the center or in a special alcove? Does it have a soft mat or a chair for you to use? Sit or lie down in the center of this space and consciously open to the lighted photons of love from the atmosphere around you. The more vividly you imagine the photons, the more real they become.

Love comes in waves, just as the ocean waves roll in. As you lie or sit very quietly and listen, imagine these waves of love rolling over you, calming your emotions, calming your mind, healing and re-energizing your body, and restoring full vitality to any organs which have been overworked or stressed.

As you breathe deeply, think of the part of you that is divine. You can experience a wave of love every time the photons of love enter your heart center. Continue to absorb these photons that make up the radiance of love. These particles of lighted love hold the secret of those who seem eternally young, and whose eyes reveal the joy quietly dancing in their hearts.

Now imagine that you can see yourself as the higher guides see you. Rather than having a physical body, imagine yourself in a body made entirely of streams of different colors. Project your imagination into the past and see behind you a being composed of the same colors that you were made of. Now sense yourself as a being composed of colors, beginning with ten years ago. Now look at yourself eight years ago, six years ago and four years ago. Notice how much brighter and clearer the colors have become with each passing year. Let this being made of colors move up toward you as it goes forward in time. Notice how much love has now been absorbed as the colors continue to become brighter.

Watch this being made up of colors move right past you and walk forward into your future. Notice how much more clear, vivid and beautiful each color becomes. What new colors are appearing? Is there a soft rich rose, a vivid green, a pale violet? Begin to get a sense of the profound love that you are learning as a result of your experiences throughout this lifetime. Observe the ease with which these colors are radiating into a greater space and embracing larger groups of people. See this being of bright clear colors freely and effortlessly extending love to others without the need to control, yet transforming and healing everyone it touches in some way.

Now imagine yourself in your earth body radiating with the same colors, and see your incredible beauty and grace as you receive and express love. You may notice the boundaries of who you thought you were seeming to dissolve. Listen for the sound of inner harmony as you see yourself talking to and working with others in this vibration of pure love.

Every time you repeat this process its effect will be even more powerful. When you feel fully complete with this visualization, leave your temple and return your focus to the room where you are sitting, feeling rejuvenated and refreshed.

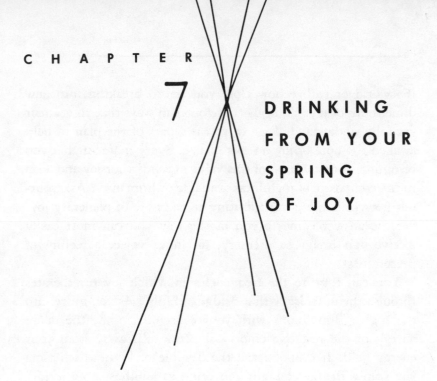

CHAPTER

7

DRINKING
FROM YOUR
SPRING
OF JOY

JAIWA Joy is the next major soul quality now available through the power of your Bridge of Light to it. Many of you are trying to reconcile the idea of being joyful with all the suffering and uncertainty in the world. You may want your life to reflect serious purpose and compassion for others. You can experience great joy *and* follow your highest principles of spiritual understanding. Your joy comes from connecting people with light, serving others, creating order and harmony around you. Someone may have told you that it is not spiritual to be joyful when there is so much global suffering. But it is in a state of joy that you make the most transforming connections with other people, send the most powerful energies of healing, lift people's spirits, and are the most creative.

You may not yet fully appreciate how valuable your joy is to the world or realize how close you are to breaking into new dimensions of joy. Your joy contributes in ways that you cannot yet fully understand. Each of you is a part of the plan to help awaken the note of joy on this planet. Every moment that you bring in a consciousness of this value expands your joy and adds to the composite of joyfulness available to humanity. Ask yourself how your life is contributing to the note of planetary joy. Let the answer come to you in the way you can most easily receive—an image, a memory, an inner voice, a feeling of peacefulness.

You can tune to the frequencies in which joy reverberates through the universe with a Bridge of Light. As you move into the higher dimensions with your conscious mind, the dense energy of the negative emotional plane falls away from your energy field. It cannot reach the Temple of Light. Each time you spin a Bridge of Light you bring in another surge of joy. This happens because you are expanding, and joy is found in outward and upward movement.

Joy is a lingering sound within the heart.

Think of joy as the melody that plays itself without an instrument. Look within the depths of your heart and you will find joy waiting for you on your Bridge of Light. Joy is playful like the wind. Breathing deeply allows the sound of joy to reverberate through your body and spirit. You have felt it many times when you were dancing to harmonious music, twirling around, or singing to yourself.

Sometimes happiness and joy go together, but happiness alone comes and goes as swiftly as the wind, and often depends on something so simple as what kind of music you are listening to, a memory that comes to mind, how your child did at school, or whether your boss is cross or gentle. One moment of happiness can transform itself into a moment of unhappiness and back again very quickly. Each state seems absolutely real—until it disappears and its opposite takes over.

The awareness of joy lies underneath the feelings of happiness or unhappiness, pleasure or pain, serenity or struggle. When you are in a state of joy you give it to others by direct transmission, without awareness of what is happening. You are simply being yourself, delighting in the adventure of life.

Even if joy goes so deep underground that it seems to be gone, it will always bubble up when the covering of any negative emotion is lifted. The expansive sense of self that joy brings often follows a courageous moment of facing doubt or indecision, sadness or loneliness. There is an open space after such feelings emerge, and in that open space the awareness of real joy can come to the surface.

If you should ever lose touch with the joy inherent in your being, work or play with someone who emanates joy to reestablish that rhythm of thinking and feeling. Try learning from many different types of people and then weaving just the right pattern of stillness and activity, of outward and inner focus, that gives you a grander experience of joy.

Music may be a rapid route to joy. The music that lifts your spirit can be a booster to keep you aware of its energy once you have made the connection. Experiencing great music is like walking on your Bridge of Light to joy as you go through the day's work. The power is not only in the sound of the music but in the joyful focus of the musicians who are playing the instruments.

LAUNA *I discovered the power of imaginative play recently while teaching mothers about the power of joy. At our October meeting I asked each person to write down* one experience of joy she desired to experience on February 26, the day before our last meeting. Then we constructed a Bridge of Light to our chosen date. Everyone forgot about this exercise by the time of our last meeting on February 27, until Martha, one of the members of the group, happened to describe the most profound and joyful connection she had ever had with her husband, the day before. Suddenly someone remembered the exercise and reminded the group. Each recalled her experience of the day before and described a different encounter with joy. None of us could remember what we had written, so we brought out the cards that we had written describing our specific wish.

Martha had described her desire for a joyous connection with her husband. To our amazement, everyone had realized the experience of joy she had imagined and described on the card. In each case the experience came as a total surprise, a spontaneous moment that seemed to happen out of the blue. One mother had wanted to feel a joyful bond with her son, and she remembered that she had been in tears with the power of the connection she had felt with him for the past three days. Another had written about a desire to wake up on that date and feel vitalized, energized, and powerful in every cell of her body. She told us that the night before she was coming down with a bad cold. Yet she woke up feeling wonderful, with no sign of anything but good energy. Our lighthearted game of creating our future had worked precisely as we had visualized by describing an experience we wanted and setting a date to experience it.

Now in my classes I encourage the members to mark their calendars with a date and a context to experience joy. They choose a date a few weeks in the future and turn it over to their Higher Selves to work out with their unconscious minds. We set dates to experience the quality of joy and know that our Bridges of Light to joy operate outside of our awareness and bring it to us. We may have forgotten the date by the time it comes around, but our unconscious mind does not forget. It delivers at the first opportunity on that date that we are open to receive.

EXERCISE
CREATING JOY IN YOUR FUTURE

Set several dates for an experience of joy and describe the experience you wish. Make it as rich as your imagination can create. Add an outrageous note, something that you rarely do. Here's an example.

> March 12: Surprised by joy. Woke up feeling light and humorous. Found myself dancing around the kitchen as I cooked breakfast.
>
> March 18: Started singing in the shower. Called my old friend ———— (or my former wife, husband, boss) to say how much value I received from our connection.
>
> March 21: Just before going to sleep, I felt a mix of joy and humor and started laughing out loud. I am still me, with all my crazy tendencies, but I felt a burst of joy simply to be alive and learning on this planet now.

Mark the calendar and your own description of joy beside the date. Then from your temple spin a Bridge of Light to joy and connect it with each of these dates. Make the bridge strong enough that you sense its energy going into the days you have marked in the future. Then forget all about it, and let yourself be surprised when the joy you have connected to your future walks into your present.

EXERCISE
ENERGIZING YOUR FRIENDS WITH JOY

Joy gets stronger and more stable as each cell in the body and mind is permeated with its specific vibration. When joy is bubbling up, its imprint is left on whatever or whomever you touch—as clearly as your signature on a letter. As you absorb the rhythm and vibrational sounds of joy, your voice picks up a richer overtone. Others may recognize the sound of joy in your voice before you do. The overtone is registered on the inner ear and responded to from the heart. Rather than try to make your voice *sound* joyful, you can embrace a symbol for joy in your temple and absorb its sound. In this exercise you can do just that.

Begin by engaging your greatest tool—your imagination—as you take a relaxed and comfortable position in your temple. Imagine a column of luminous light encircling you as you breathe deeply. Hold the air in your lungs for several seconds and imagine this light permeating the air sacs in your lungs, cleansing and recharging them.

Think about what joy is, about its power to transform people's lives, about its many possibilities of expression, such as music, color, and sound. Engage your heart's passion. What do you love doing, seeing, sensing, or hearing that could be in your life right now? Plan a way to make more time available for it. Imagine that your thoughts are adding to the force field of joy and making its healing energy more available for anyone on the planet to draw from.

Recall memories of a few of your most joyous experiences. Notice what happens to your breathing as you remember each scene as vividly as possible, how you stood or sat, the sounds around you, the colors in the room or in nature, the people present, what you said, how you felt. Sharpen the picture of them until your breathing deepens and you experience that joy again.

Many symbols of true joy are stored in your memory bank. Select an image that symbolizes joy for you (a flower, a star, a tall pine tree). Enliven the image that comes to you by talking to it, dancing with it, in some way bringing it near to you.

Now spin a Bridge of Light to joy. Think of your symbol as an instrument that taps into the electromagnetic particles of joy and connects them to you. Sense the luminous radiance around the symbol. Let its luminosity become brighter. Listen for its sound.

Next, imagine a group of people standing shoulder to shoulder in a circle, facing into the center. You can include a circle of nine or ten friends and later you can add to it until you have 100 or more in your circle. Imagine that your symbol of joy is circling the room and impressing each person with its energy. See the smiles of the people as they feel the spirit of joy come over them.

Imagine these people as they go to bed tonight, climbing into their beds with a peaceful smile on their faces as they fall asleep.

You can create the circle using any quality—harmony, joy, wisdom, truth—whatever you sense is most needed. Include larger or smaller circles, and notice the delight in your own life expanding as joy reverberates between you and your circle of friends.

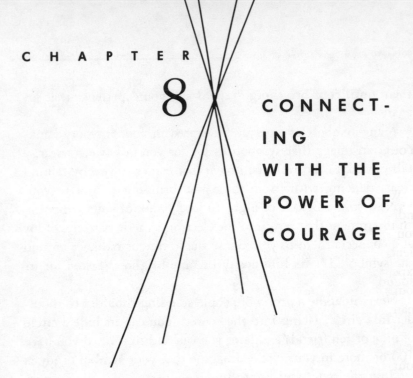

CHAPTER

8

CONNECT-ING WITH THE POWER OF COURAGE

LAUNA The third spiritual quality that dramatically expands our life energy is courage. There are so many things that we feel directed to do, yet they sometimes appear to be too challenging for the skills and capacities we think we have. Many people have a wonderful dream or vision. Why is it that so few people actually carry out their higher purpose and visions? Jaiwa says that the single most important quality that would empower people to make their dreams come true and to express their higher purpose is the quality of courage.

JAIWA

Your first act of courage was to be born on this planet.

When you were born, you chose to express yourself as an individual, separate from the womb of cosmic energy. Each of you left the security of cosmic consciousness to gain the experience of yourself as an individual, and to learn from your experiences how to use the light of your essence on earth. Your courage to express a greater wisdom and love powerfully affects many people, including many you may never meet.

Since then you have been courageous many times. You may be able to look back now and see some of the courageous acts of your life. We see them. They are clearly recorded in your energy field. You might call them the turning points of your life, the times when you took a step toward becoming what you knew you could be, as a result of an inner vision. You may have done this in spite of strong objections from family or friends, removing yourself from an atmosphere that was pleasant, but which kept you lulled in a kind of sleep. You may have moved into new territory within, or perhaps in the outside world to another state or city, perhaps without money, job, or family. Or you may have made an inner move in which you switched your consciousness to another dimension of who you were. Often the two go hand in hand; a physical move often follows an expansion of consciousness. Sometimes adding a room to your house or creating a garden is a symbolic move. Even painting the front door a new color is a symbol of courageously acknowledging more of who you are.

Imagine which courageous acts in your life would be recorded in a cosmic life record book.

Imagine that a detailed record of your courageous acts and decisions is being kept. It records every occasion when you did not take the easy way or the familiar path, but responded with courage to a unique call within yourself. It may not have been a dramatic moment, but was nevertheless a decision that changed the direction of your life. You may not have felt especially courageous when you made the choice. You may have felt trapped or scared to death. Others may have considered you disobedient, stubborn, or rebellious, but you took the courageous step anyway. Think of several that would probably be in this book.

These acts were all leading up to your decision to learn more about your Higher Self and to expand into more light. The fear of being criticized or made fun of or of looking foolish falls away when you have the courage to simply express your radiant self. Courage erases old patterns of fear. They were there to protect you until you found a sense of direction toward the light. Now it is safe to dissolve them with the soul quality of courage.

You need not be a Joan of Arc or a Galileo in order to express courage. The results of bringing in courage may be different for each of you. One person may use courage to experience the camaraderie of groups more frequently, while another uses it to go within and experience the divinity of her own true self. You may have used courage in making a move toward your dream; you may have left behind traditional pictures of financial security or the security of family and friends. Each such move takes great courage. The familiar ways are always the easiest to follow, and a new direction is always the most challenging.

Think of courage as wisdom and compassion brought together. True courage results in a steady and persistent intelligent action to bring about what has true value to you. Each time you act with courage, you empower your entire life. And you also empower others who can see the positive direction and purpose of your courage.

LAUNA *We often miss how much we influence others by doing what seems perfectly natural to us rather than by any effort to be courageous. One day I overheard a remark by a 90-year-old professional photographer as she explained to a friend that she worked out in the mornings at her ballet barre before beginning her photography assignments. I suddenly realized that I too could be a blithe spirit in mind and body at 90 instead of the fragile old woman I had unconsciously been imagining. I immediately converted my old pictures, and every time they come to mind, I refocus and consciously replace them with a vivid picture of the vigorous, energetic photographer whose courage is simply her way of being. Overhearing a simple statement gave me what a thousand lectures or treatments could not—a living example of vitality and creativity. That photographer may not know that being extraordinarily agile and creative in her nineties is a form of courage, much less that she is offering courage to anyone else. She simply pulled away from the familiar role of an old woman and is courageously living according to a higher picture which feels to her like a perfectly natural way to live.*

JAIWA

Every time you act from courage, you strengthen your ability to live by the authority of your own soul.

When you bring in more courage, the chances are you will not immediately notice it as such. It will seem as if you are doing what comes naturally—assuming your equality in spirit with every human being on the planet. It seems like a paradox, but you can be less secure in the physical world, yet still be happier and more creative. You have a sense that you will be able to bring in enough money to take care of your needs and that you will connect with the kind of people whose energy resonates with your own.

Courage brings new possibilities into your life. It gives you a new way of looking at the world. To imagine the source and the power of courage, see it as a grand entity radiating like the sun. You can connect with its energy by spinning a Bridge of Light to it from your heart center. It becomes available as the new frequencies on your bridge activate the brain cells which can resonate with its powerful vibration. When you feel confident and expectant of success, it means that your courage is one degree or more stronger than any sense of apathy or fear. That's all you need to see a greater truth from the vibration of your soul and act on it.

Once you sense how much difference courage would make in your life, you have already started the changes. You can find the courage to ask for what you need, to be honest where you have felt compelled to cover the truth, to speak where you were silent, even to explore new possibilities that once seemed over your head. As you take the first step, courage to do more will be close behind.

LAUNA A *client who came to me was having a lot of trouble handling her teenage sons. First, I showed her how to exaggerate her fear by taking a crouched* posture in a corner of the room. Then she called in courage by taking an exaggerated posture of courage, walking around the room, and talking with force and power. In each position she immediately experienced the feelings that went with it. She realized she could bring in the feeling that she wanted by simply taking the position and stance of that feeling. The next time her sons rebelled against a house rule she would take the stance of courage, build a Bridge of Light to it, and begin to speak. What surprised her was how gentle she could be with them once she had called in her courage. (Without the inner strength that the courage gave her, she could shout and yell without any results.) After that, as soon as she felt fearful about taking a firm position, she would remember the two postures and consciously choose the courageous one. She learned to construct a Bridge of Light to the quality of courage with her eyes wide open if the need arose—and found in the process a new level of confidence.

Sometimes it takes courage to decline an honor. A friend in Chicago was offered the presidency of a large nonprofit institution, a coveted honor for any of the city's leaders. She did not fear the job, but when she turned to her most probable future in it, the job felt tedious, full of long committee meetings and obligatory dinners. She decided to turn the offer down, but before she called the foundation chairman to say so, she sat very quietly and constructed a Bridge of Light to the pure energy of courage. Something shifted in her mind. Instead of making polite excuses, she called and told him honestly about her sense of the job, the busywork involved, the lack of power to make real changes, and what she thought the board of directors needed to change immediately. The chairman of the board was so impressed with her honest approach, her courage to say no if she couldn't be effective, and her intuitive observations that he agreed to make the changes in the job, free her from several committees, and support her in making the changes she suggested. She said yes—and meant it wholeheartedly. "This job," she said, "is a great opportunity for me to learn how to bring courage into a new and challenging situation, and I love it."

There are stories of courage in everyone's life. A friend, Joan, describes coming to California with her small child and a friend, without a job, a husband, or a place to live, and amid serious objections from her family. "I knew I had to change my entire focus and leave my supportive family atmosphere in order to grow and expand," she says. "I had a sense of 'Anything is possible' and it was. I married a fine man and together we have created the family life we wanted." Joan is preparing a kit for schoolchildren that will use symbols to help them make a connection with their Higher Selves. "I never would have started this ambitious venture without the earlier experience of using courage to let go of a life that was very easy for something that was exciting and challenging."

Anytime you get very clear and committed to something, you will find the courage to do it. Courage is easier when you have a sense of real purpose. The courage to say no, to say yes, to begin again, or to let go of something comes when there is a sense of real meaning in doing so.

A friend decided he wanted to help feed the hungry people of the world. He soon became active in a private nonprofit program called SHARE. This group offers food packages at a low price to people who need assistance. My friend built many Bridges of Light to the quality of courage before initiating the program in a new city. Once when more funds were needed, he had a sense of three people appearing on the bridge and signaling that they had come to help. Sure enough, the financial needs were dissolved within a brief time by a new cadre of volunteers. Today SHARE has more than 135,000 families around the world participating in the program. "Each expansion we make requires new levels of courage," he says, "yet this work is the most heart-filling work I can imagine."

A CHECK FOR COURAGE

Compare your courage now with your courage five years ago.

Use the following chart to compare your courage now with your courage five years ago and the level of courage you desire six months from now. Use a scale of 1 to 10, with 1 representing almost no expression of courage and 10 meaning a very powerful expression of it. Consider even a one-point increase a significant step forward. Fill in today's date, so you can see the difference the next time you open to this chapter. Before you fill in the last column, stop and imagine how it would feel to express courage at the level you desire. If you can imagine it, you can do it.

If you have not consciously realized that you are beginning to express the quality of courage, reflect on these six opportunities to express courage and see how far you have come. Each experience (including the most delightful) can increase your courage to act from your true attributes rather than from habit.

In two weeks, check the list again and notice the areas where you are making new leaps in courage. Acknowledge this expansion to one or two friends, and yet another leap in courage will be freed to appear.

Each time you allow the light of your essence to flow into your life, you are integrating another level of courage and making this new level more available to many others—both people you know and people you don't know. An extrasensory knowing acts as a grapevine communication around the planet.

When enough people begin to express any higher quality it becomes much more available to others.

	Five years ago	Now	Six months from now
1. Courage to ask your Higher Self to show you everything that stands in the way of your highest expression.			
2. Courage to say no to requests for your time or energy that you have no interest in.			
3. Courage to meet with your Higher Self and to open to its love and wisdom.			
4. Courage to acknowledge a beautiful trait in someone, even someone you do not know well.			
5. Courage to consciously allow pictures to emerge that represent the future closest to your heart and to believe in those pictures.			
6. Courage to see yourself as a radiant being of light.			

EXERCISE
SYNCHRONIZING OTHER QUALITIES
WITH COURAGE

W hen a conflict arises or a challenge presents itself, there is a great additional power in synchronizing one quality with another. If your job is threatened by a coworker, you may need courage, but also truth and compassion to handle the situation in a way that will be honest and straightforward yet warm and accepting. If you see a way to bring new prosperity, love, or wisdom into your life, you may need several qualities along with courage before you can act on it.

Select a situation now where courage would make a grand difference. Imagine that the situation you are thinking of is being transferred from your mind to your left hand. You can feel this hand receiving it even as you read.

Choose to experience courage as a distinct quality, different from love, truth, or joy. Feel its flow in and out of your heart, as regular as your heartbeat itself.

From your temple, spin a Bridge of Light to courage and continue to add strands of light until you feel the strength of your bridge and sense it taking the shape of a bridge to another dimension.

Next, take some very deep breaths and imagine your body and mind filled with the pure essence of courage. Taste its distinctive flavor. Close your eyes and say the word "courage" to yourself several times. Imagine that it is penetrating all the cells in your body, entering into your circulatory system, and becoming a biochemical part of your blood.

When you feel that your pulse is beating with the vibration of courage, touch your throat with the fingers of your *right* hand to feel this powerful pulse.

Imagine another quality, such as understanding, which also

has its own separate radiance, and allow it to inundate your mind and body in the same way. Again, touch the pulse at your throat with your fingers.

Bring in humor and love—or whatever will be most helpful in the situation you are dealing with. When you feel that its energy is pulsing through your body, touch your throat at its pulsing center again. At this point you have brought together the energy of several distinctive qualities.

Now, very slowly bring your left hand to the pulse at your throat and touch it in exactly the place that you touched it with the qualities of courage, understanding, humor, and love. Close your eyes and pause for a moment as you inhale deeply while the neuron transfers take place in your brain.

Imagine the situation now and see what has been created by the changes. Do you feel more energized as you think of it? Does it feel more possible to handle? Is there an ease of taking action visible to you? What ideas do you see that could make the situation one that will bring you an abundance of delight?

You are symbolically bringing the qualities into the situation so that they will transform the energy of the situation itself. New ideas may continue to drop into your mind as you go through the day. As your new response spreads to similar situations, understanding, humor, and courage will come to-gether as a package into other situations whenever you need them.

SECTION III

CREATING A SOUL- INFUSED PERSONALITY

Now it is time for the practical work of handling every problem, challenge, and crisis that comes up in your life. You will be practicing using an essence detection device to discern which goals are coming from personality desires and which ones are essence- or soul-inspired. You will find methods and techniques here to integrate all the sides of your personality and bring them into a finer balance with the light, learn how to handle fears with the spiritual quality of trust, and release or change certain memories of your past. In the last chapter you will learn how to keep a balanced and sound mind while you infuse your personality with greater light.

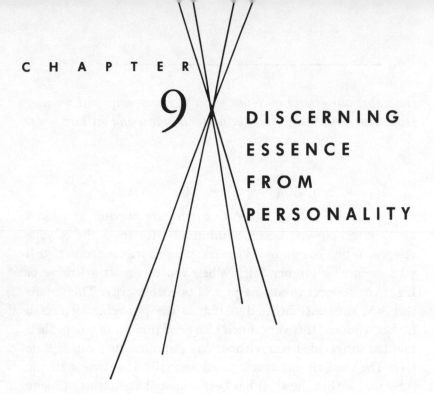

CHAPTER

9

DISCERNING

ESSENCE

FROM

PERSONALITY

LAUNA How do we tell which of our driving urges to succeed, to relate to someone, to own land or a home, to travel, or to change jobs is a soul urge that will expand us into greater light and love, and which is an old personality ambition that will limit us from the kind of expansion we want? How can we know whether we are tapping into our intuitive wisdom when we go after something, or simply responding to patterns that were begun by unconscious beliefs set in our personality when we were very small?

While our Higher Self is channeling clarity and light into our lives, what is happening with our personality? Sometimes it can react with very strong objections, much as a jealous child might react when its mother is talking with a friend. It is still working on goals that we are losing interest in. Once we have opened to

the light, old desires may not seem so important, and we may
sense that something very important is missing in our lives.

JAIWA We who are serving as guides
are here to help you become luminous with the light of your
essence. When you go into your temple you are connecting with
your essence or Higher Self. When you construct a Bridge of
Light you connect to some aspect of essence energy. This means
that you are constantly adjusting to the powerful force of a
higher wisdom. It is very much like breaking out of an eggshell
that has surrounded you without any assurance that you will be
safe. The shell simply cracks open and falls away when all the
substance within the shell has been digested as a result of many
experiences. When the mind is strong enough to handle the
new environment, the shell is no longer needed. Appreciate the
excitement of the new environment that awaits you even as you
feel the first cracks in the shell that has existed for so long as a
protection to your mind.

Your formless essence is the source of your consciousness.

What we guides refer to as formless essence, soul, or Higher
Self is the source of your consciousness. The life of the soul is
lived in a different dimension of reality than your personality,
although it has often responded to your personality in times of
emergencies. Meditation opens the door to the soul's wisdom
and love, but unless the door is consciously opened each day,
even if only for a few minutes, most people's souls are able to
reach and assist their personalities only in times of great need.
In the midst of an extreme crisis, the soul's essence can infuse
the personality with the wisdom and understanding necessary to

handle the emergency. It is a moment of great truth when the personality surrenders its control and turns to the soul for direction. A great light floods the person's entire being for as long as the soul is in charge. These times of soul intervention happen not only in emergencies of physical danger, but also in times when you are deciding your direction in life, or choosing a new philosophy from which to live.

But you can consult with and learn from your Higher or Essence Self every day, each time becoming more aware of its slower vibration. This vibration activates dormant brain cells every time you connect with it, and as this happens you awaken to greater truth, purpose, and understanding. Each time you enter your Temple of Light and communicate with your Higher Self, you add another strand of light to the bridge between your soul and your personality.

Think of your Essence Self as the snow on top of the tallest mountain, pure and dazzling, reflecting the light of the sun. As a portion of the snow melts, it forms streams and waterfalls, which splash down the mountainside and into the valley below. Those streams are the various aspects of your personality. Your body, mind, and emotions are the major rivers formed by the streams as they rush down the mountain. Just as the snow is the source of every mountain stream, your formless essence is the source of every aspect of your personality. But the qualities of the personality change as it gets farther and farther away from its source, just as the quality of water changes, losing some of its sweetness and sparkling clarity, as the mountain streams run to the valley floor.

The mountain rivers and their tributaries are formed from only a small part of the mountain's snow, just as your personality is only a small part of the divine being that is you. The Essence Self remembers everything, but the personality forgets that its source is from a higher power.

We guides watch you struggling to handle the fast pace that

your personalities set up. They set up goals, especially those which offer "more" of something. They love new self-discipline programs—becoming thin, becoming fit, becoming young. The personality likes to trade, bargain, compare, forgive, and try to love; it wants to be good, be liked, be powerful, purposeful, and peaceful. The more challenging the goal, the more intrigued the personality. But personality goals can make claims on energy that is not there for them, and it is easy for your personality to begin borrowing energy from your basic life force with a vague promise to pay back soon. Personalities have great skills and information, yet without the influx of essence energy, they are seriously handicapped.

Your Essence Self has different priorities and its work is very different from that of the personality. It is the doorway to the loving acceptance of the true value of your life. Essence energy doesn't forgive, it simply sees there is no forgiveness necessary. It does not take life so seriously as your personality does; it sees this lifetime as an adventure of learning, of joy and expansion.

You can distinguish between personality goals and essence work by carefully noting who is to benefit. Essence-inspired work benefits more than one person; often it affects large groups of people either directly or indirectly. Your essence work has a unique sound which attracts the energy of other Higher Selves, whose notes join the sound of yours. The resulting symphony is sounded above the spectrum of physical hearing. These harmonious tones create a powerful sound that empowers each goal conceived in the higher vibration.

A new quality comes into your work when this happens, far more powerful than you alone could have created. Doors open, people come, others assist, a group forms of like minds and spirits. Coincidences happen which seem to be orchestrated from some other place—connecting with information, people, money, and the tools needed. A sense of harmony can happen even when there are varying personal viewpoints; people cooperate who would not be drawn together unless there was a higher purpose in the work. Their personalities may be so diverse that if the goal were coming from personality interest alone, these people would not be working together.

Essence-inspired goals give you energy.

Essence goals derive from the larger vision for your life and the meaning you derive from it. When the radiance of your essence is in the heart of a goal, you feel an inner urge to keep going. Even if the work involved is unexpectedly demanding, an inner urge motivates you to push onward. The feeling is different from self-discipline. You can tap into a regenerating source of new energy to complete essence-inspired work. It keeps the flame of clear intention alive even while the soup is cooking and the bills are being paid.

When you are immersed in essence energy, feeling its peace and tranquility, you can see anything that is blocking your true creativity, and choose a different response. If you realize that trying to do too many things at once is blocking your rhythm of creative work, for example, you can consciously cut down on your activities and leave more energy for the work that resonates with your Higher Self. Finally, at some point there comes a switch in consciousness, and the flow of creative, productive work becomes steady and powerful.

LAUNA W*henever you are pushing yourself and your life feels like a continual struggle, you can guess that you are off your highest path for that hour or day. When this happens to me, I am learning to stop and take a break, begin to breathe in a deeper rhythm, and enter my temple. The* minute I step across the threshold, I am immersed in a completely different sense of myself, and after a few minutes of absorbing the peace there, my work for that section of the day becomes clear. Often I am surprised at how simple a job can be—once my personality opens to other ideas that are inherent in the new energy.

If a feeling of struggle persists, carefully check the method you are using to reach your higher goal. A dedicated spiritual friend inherited some money and began to study the stock market every day in an effort to increase her holdings so she could begin a healing center in her town. Even though she dreaded getting up every morning and studying detailed corporation charts, she kept plodding along month after month. For two or three years she had good profits. Yet keeping up with the market was taking more and more of her time. She thought of getting out but couldn't bring herself to let go. Suddenly the market crashed and she lost all of her gains—and much more. She confided that the method she had chosen to increase her funds was a decision to go with the "experts." Top financial advisers told her what to do, and she listened to them, even though her inner voice repeatedly showed her a picture of stormy seas ahead.

In spite of the outcome—five years of her time and energy seemingly wasted—she realized that she had learned an important lesson. Had she not immersed herself exclusively in "expert" advice about how to handle her money, and lost, she would have always been inclined to go with the experts regardless of her own intuition. She also realized that if she had not lost so much, she would have trapped herself in stock market speculations indefinitely instead of beginning the healing center with what she had.

It is important to learn to withhold judgment on what may appear to be a selfish goal. Sometimes what seems to be a personality goal will keep coming up and urging you to act on *it. In an opposite kind of case, a friend in Mill Valley, Joy Watson, almost rejected a desire that was actually very important to her. She wanted to spend a week alone. It seemed like a selfish personality goal, but it became more important to her than anything else. Finally she decided to honor this inner need, and left for a week alone with the full support of her husband and teenage daughter. In that week of doing what she wanted to do—taking walks, sitting by a river, forgetting her family and responsibilities—she was able to enter her Temple of Light and absorb its gifts so totally that she began to develop new ideas for an organization she was founding called Mind Fitness, International. She has just returned from Moscow where she presented her plans to an enthusiastic audience of Russians at the Academy of Scientists. She says her week of connecting with her Essence Self was one of the most valuable weeks of her life.*

TOOL OF LIGHT
CREATING AN ESSENCE DETECTION
DEVICE

Get a notebook or fresh sheet of paper and a pen. Read through the following instructions first and then do the different parts of the exercise.

1. Close your eyes, breathe deeply at least seven times, remembering to tighten and relax your muscles, bring your shoulders to your ears, and roll your neck from side to side. Be aware of crossing the meadow, climbing the mountain, and opening the door of your temple as you step inside.
2. Imagine that inside the temple you have an essence detection device which can measure the precise degree of essence in any thought, goal, or relationship, and show this measure of essence to you as a number, a color, or a symbol. Decide to play with the detector for a few minutes. Ask the rational side of your

brain to allow the superconscious through while you play.

3. You can picture your detector having a 1 to 10 digital readout if you like numbers, or a gemstone brilliance scale if you like symbols. If you prefer colors, look for the clear, vivid colors to show the essence-filled work you are doing. Expect the response to each question to be instantaneous. The answers come through your intuition and bypass your logical reasoning mind.

4. Stop reading right here and list your most important goals without stopping to censor. Check each goal you have listed by mentally setting the essence detector over it. Write whatever number or symbol comes to mind without stopping to think. Like any skill, the process of checking your goals for their essence quality will become sharper and more precise with practice.

5. The essence detector can print other useful information on your mind screen. Ask for a signal light flashing red or green to show you the most likely outcome of an anticipated action or a situation you are already involved in. (The Higher Self knows far more than people have realized.) When you set up the opportunity for this intuitive knowing to come through, it will.

TOOL OF LIGHT
SHIFTING A PERSONALITY GOAL WITH ESSENCE ENERGY

You can take a project or goal that is personality-based and transform it with a specific quality from your essence. Again, the energy of your Temple of Light assures the success of this experiment, so enter it first as you practiced in Chapter 3.

Once inside, choose a personality project, such as cleaning a closet, reorganizing your desk, or updating your wardrobe. Put it in your left hand with the power of your imagination. Talk to it for a few minutes if it helps you to identify its presence in that hand. When it is in place, choose an essence quality that might work a small miracle on it—for example, lightness, humor, patience, clarity, wisdom, or beauty. Imagine that the essence quality you have chosen is in your right hand. Concentrate on its presence there until your right hand tingles or becomes warmer.

Next, actually hold your hands up, facing each other, with fingers together and pointing up, about two feet apart. Very slowly begin to bring your hands together, an inch at a time. Imagine a ball of light between them as you move them closer together. Finally, bring both hands together and hold them there for a moment.

Think about the personality project again and notice its new direction and how effortlessly you can accomplish it. It may have dissolved completely, or it may seem even more important, but it most certainly will bring you far greater rewards now than before you enriched and enlivened it with a specific essence quality.

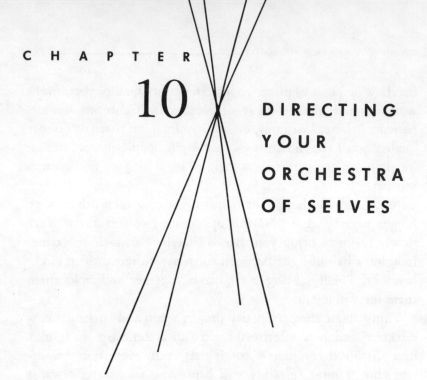

CHAPTER

10

DIRECTING
YOUR
ORCHESTRA
OF SELVES

LAUNA Have you noticed that sometimes, just after you have made a strong connection with your Higher Self, something within gets stirred up and causes trouble? Different sides of our personalities can play havoc with our sense of peace and serenity. One side may judge us, another may analyze what we are doing and criticize it. We may have a side of ourselves that wants to play all day and another part that thinks we should work all the time. Or we may have a gloomy side playing opposite a side that acts cheerful and buoyant. These sides can cause confusion and misery if they gain control—because they feel like they are us. We call these different aspects of the self our subpersonalities.

What happens as we expand is that the higher vibration of light illumines our mind each time we meditate—but it also *energizes all the parts of our personalities which are not yet integrated into the core personality self. Stimulated by the light, they get stronger, demand more attention, and want more control. The less developed subpersonalities can make our lives seem crazier than ever. We can get very confused about who we are with all of these parts of ourselves claiming to be "I." As soon as one steps in front of our mind's lens, it begins affecting our moods and decisions. At that moment, we see the world through its eyes, rather than through the eyes of our true self.*

J A I W A

One of the major challenges in the new light is to learn how to handle subpersonalities.

Subpersonalities can literally cut off the rays of light from your mind. Every time you say "I am angry" or "I am hurt," you give them more power. If you say, instead, "There is a little part of me that is reacting with anger" (or hurt, or confusion, or jealousy, or fear) you are reclaiming the position of your central self which has direct access to the Higher Self and its light.

Subpersonalities are not real, but until you see that they are not you, they will seem very real. Think of your subpersonalities as the displays in a holography exhibit. A three-dimensional holo-gram of a dancer looks solid. It seems to move as you walk around it, but if you reach out to touch it, your hand goes right through it. The dancer is an illusion created with photography. She only appears to be real. Subpersonalities—even those which feel most anxious or guilty—are no more solid than a hologram. They represent habitual patterns of the brain, just as the hologram represents patterns of light focused on film. It's a feat of courage to let go of thinking they are your real self without actually seeing anything beyond them at that moment that *is* real.

Each subpersonality has an opposite one to create a sense of balance. As you observe each subpersonality more closely, you discover that there is always another with an opposing view. It may have less force and be fairly quiescent in the shadows, but it will be around somewhere. They are the actors in the drama of your life and your central personality self is the director. Your Higher Self, or essence, or soul, is the author.

The first thing to do is to recognize the major subpersonalities that influence your decisions. Each one represents a set way of thinking or feeling that has become so familiar it is virtually automatic. None of these subpersonalities is against you; each of them is trying to help you. But some of them simply don't know how to help.

Each subpersonality has its own distinctive characteristics. The ones which you are most likely to resist are the negative ones—which surface as angry, resentful, jealous, afraid, selfish, judgmental, or just plain lazy. Some subpersonalities are altruistic. They want to be wise and giving, but they need the clarity and discrimination of the Higher Self to carry out their good intentions.

The subpersonality in control at the moment determines how you think and relate to the world. Often, the view through a particular subpersonality is quite distorted. If you realize it's a subpersonality instead of your real self, you can smile or laugh as you do when you see your distorted image in a funhouse mirror at the fair. Humor helps you regain your perspective of your true self.

All your subpersonalities are trying to help you.

Although some aspects of your personality are not helpful, all are *trying* to help. Each of their goals is about protecting you from being hurt or disappointed or looking foolish. Their criticisms are meant to help you; their judgments to warn you. Since each subpersonality has its own individual goals, it believes it is helping when it criticizes or sets up guilty feelings, or when it is "justifiably" angry, sullen, vengeful, or jealous.

Subpersonalities respond very positively to friendship and direction. One of the first ones you can retrain is the critical or judgmental one. That's the one that finds fault with the way you are handling your life and doesn't hesitate to point out specifics. The critical or judgmental subpersonality blocks joy and delight more than any outside limitation.

The best way to establish harmony is to call in your Higher Self. Left to their own resources, your subpersonalities will always be in conflict, even though that conflict is usually invisible. But any time you identify more strongly with your Higher Self than with one of your subpersonalities, your thinking and feeling shift to a higher vibration. As one man put it, "Finally, I can get past all the little gremlins and ghouls that have threatened and bullied me since I was a child." He learned to bring each of his subpersonalities to his Temple of Light— one at a time.

Encourage each subpersonality to work for you.

Since all subpersonalities are created by the mind, you can coach them to use their skills in ways that are truly helpful. You can focus on any of your subpersonalities and analyze them, diagnose them, cajole them, excuse them, or berate them, but they learn best from encouragement and a new vision.

Teach them to understand and cooperate with your vision, and with each other. As you establish a working relationship with your subpersonalities, the special attributes of each will become obvious. You can use them to organize your work, your physical fitness, your time schedules and appointments. Another may enjoy the precision of words and be able to help express the ideas that come from your Higher Self. Your recognition of them, your willingness to get to know them and retrain them can give them the kind of nourishment they need to change.

LAUNA

In my work with subpersonalities during the past fifteen years, I have found that the nature of these subpersonalities has no substance. They may feel like us, but they are not us. They do not share our essence. The only power they have is the power we have given to them, although we have done so unconsciously. Subpersonalities are like robots, programmed, and incapable of diverging from the program that created them until we see that we created them and then begin to work to bring each pair of opposites together. From this merging, we can absorb the energy we gave to them back into our own core self.

Here are some ways to merge your subpersonalities into your core self. Begin by getting to know the major ones. Listen to each of their needs and make an agreement with them that you can keep. Tell them your needs and vision and get their agreement to cooperate. Coach them in new ways to help you. Finally, take them to your temple and let the light of love pour over and permeate them. The power of the light working together with the guidance of your mind to bring opposite subpersonalities closer together will finally enable you to merge them and their energy into your central personality self.

I had a subpersonality which used to interrupt me just as Jaiwa's powerful, loving energy began to pour through me and I had begun to record his message. This skeptical subpersonality would say to me, "This isn't anything," or, "Everybody knows that." If I was channeling something I understood immediately, it would say, "You are just repeating what you already know."

If I was channeling something that was entirely new to me, it would say, "That is outrageous, just a wild figment of your imagination." I would hear its comments clearly, and would continue channeling and holding the finer vibration only by the strength of an inner commitment. About fifteen or twenty minutes into the channeling, its voice would begin to be softer and less skeptical, and finally it would become very quiet and listen quite respectfully.

I began to teach this subpersonality a new role. It obviously had a critical faculty and wanted to protect me from being gullible. I reviewed all of Jaiwa's work for this subpersonality and found that all the information and exercises had proved very helpful. Over and over again Jaiwa had sized up the needs of a client, or future trends, sometimes giving us dates or warnings or suggestions that would have been impossible for us to know without his help. Then I showed this subpersonality how to assist me in a better way. I asked it to be very alert for times when I could simply use good common sense to make a decision rather than tune to the higher vibration. Its resistance changed immediately. Now it is alert to perform its new role efficiently and has become a genuine supporter to Jaiwa. I keep my bargain and respond to its nudgings about using common sense.

Without exception, everyone I have worked with who has made a connection to his or her Higher Self or a guide has had times of stopping to handle a subpersonality that says he or she is making it all up. It is important to check out all questions from subpersonalities, and take an objective view to see if there is truly any validity in what they are saying. For example, if you review the information you have recorded in your telepathic receiving room of your Temple, and observe the uncanny accuracy with which your higher guidance has sized up a situation, you will be able to teach a skeptical subpersonality new respect.

You can be a powerful teacher for your subpersonalities. Here is an experience you may enjoy which could surprise you by what happens.

EXERCISE
CREATING A TRUSTING FRIENDSHIP WITH
A SUBPERSONALITY

Subpersonality Exercise

Select a time and place where you will be undisturbed for a half hour. Close your eyes and take several deep breaths as you let go of outside concerns. Connect with your Bridge of Light by imagining a column of light rising from the top of your head. Let it rise until it meets a column of light from above focused toward you. When the two lights are joined in your mind, become aware of your breathing again. Each deep, easy breath clears the column of light so that it is more luminous and transparent. Let your breathing be slow, effortless, and rhythmic.

Feel your self rising until you are standing on the Bridge of Light, in a higher dimension than the ordinary world. Imagine that you see below you a wooded area with several little houses among the trees. Choose one of the houses to visit and imagine yourself approaching it and knocking on the door. When the door is opened, one of your subpersonalities will invite you to enter. Get to know this subpersonality. Give it a name (Hazel, Jo, Rupert, Priscilla) and begin by finding out its needs. Listen to its complaints or comments about the way you have treated it. Don't let it engage you in argument or self-defense. Be gentle and understanding. You are here as a respectful guest.

Invite it to go outdoors in the sunlight and to take a walk with you. As you walk, tell it your needs, and when you feel that a trust between you is established, tell it your vision of your life and your work. Learn about its skills and how it can assist you. ("You can gently remind me to listen to my daughter when she is troubled, instead of criticizing me when I forget.")

In this walk with a subpersonality, you have the opportunity to transfuse it with light and a new vision. As you acknowledge and appreciate its skills, watch it go through changes. It may begin to look and act differently as you walk in the sunlight together. If it had a shriveled or hunched shape, it may grow taller and healthier. Its attitude will probably become more trusting and positive.

Before you leave, make an agreement with it to handle its reasonable needs and get an agreement from it to help with your needs. Be specific. If it wants you to exercise more, decide how much you are willing to exercise and still be in balance with the rest of your life. If it shows you that you are wearing your body out too fast, make a specific agreement of how you will take better care of yourself. This is a very powerful process in order to assemble all of your energies together to empower your life.

Ask yourself where in your body you have kept this entity lodged. Look for any tense patterns in the muscles of your stomach, shoulders, neck, thighs, or jaw. Imagine that it is letting go of any hold it has over your body. Its resistance to cooperating is now dissolving; as it does, your body relaxes.

EXERCISE
CREATING A CIRCLE OF YOUR
SUBPERSONALITIES

After you have taken several of your subpersonalities for a walk in the sunlight, bring all of them to your temple. Begin by imagining that they are sitting around you in a circle. Ask them to give you their pledge of commitment and loyalty to your vision. Keep asking until you can hear unanimous agreement. Then imagine that all the subpersonalities are joining hands, resonating to your vision with you. Feel your full power as they commit to the vision of your highest possible future. Touch each member of your orchestra of subselves with the brightest, purest truth you can. Stand and bask in an experience of oneness, a grand unity between all your subpersonalities and your soul.

All of the subpersonalities will be changed in some way after this meeting in your temple. Celebrate the beginning of the fusion of all their energies with you, the real director of your life.

CHAPTER

11

DISSOLVING
FEARS WITH
TRUST

LAUNA

Fears about launching a new career, moving to a new area, starting or ending a relationship, or about any big change sometimes hold us back from doing what we want to do. We don't want to push our fears underground, even if we could, but they may seem to be stronger than before we opened to more light. Their dense energy can stop us from taking action on some of our finest opportunities. How can we know when a fear is masquerading as our intuition? How can we handle fears and actually dissolve them so that we don't have to keep dealing with the same fears coming up in every new and challenging situation? These are the questions that some of you may be facing now as old fears are coming to the surface in the new intensity of light.

J A I W A

Every emotional pattern that doesn't harmonize with the higher vibration is coming up now to be healed.

Now that you are working with light in your temple, everyone you know and every situation you are involved in is here to serve your expansion. Any potentially negative situation is an opportunity to use a Bridge of Light to clear your mind and emotions as fast as possible. For example, if your work is a continuous sturggle of pointless activity, it may be off your path; a Bridge of Light can awaken you to ways to work with something you love doing. If your wife or husband is fearful about your wider approach to life, you may find new ways to express your deep love to your mate. If your child is unhappy at school you may experience a deep understanding of his or her fears and offer compassionate help and reassurance.

Emotions that stem from fear can range from sadness or depression through frustration to downright fury! The cause of all negative feelings may seem obvious—something that is happening *to* you. But the root cause of all negative emotions is nearly always a hidden pattern of *fear* coming from somewhere within you. It may be stimulated by the denser energies around you, but there has to be a matching pattern somewhere within you for it to become a problem.

Your energy field is like the home you live in.

The energy field that you have gathered around you includes all the responses to your thoughts, experiences, and feelings. These responses evolve as your ability increases to reflect the light of the soul more clearly. You create your reality system through the filter of your energy field. From this place, assumptions about yourself and your world are formed. Each thought or emotion is represented by a specific shade or color. As your mind produces thoughts, certain emotions arise in response to each one. Each emotion matches the tone of the thought. Happy or unhappy, optimistic or pessimistic—all these feelings depend upon the thought that precedes them. When the same kinds of thoughts are repeated frequently, they become a basic pattern in your energy field. They reside within the energy field that surrounds each person. They have a definite vibratory rhythm and sound and are composed of layers of colors and sounds which are ordinarily invisible and inaudible. Everyone who comes into your electromagnetic field of energy responds to the note and rhythm that is emanating from it.

Other people offer you opportunities to clear your energy field of all negative energy.

When you make a commitment to choose a life that is guided by your Higher Self instead of your personality, you begin to attract people and experiences that can help clear your energy field of once useful but now useless and restricting patterns of thinking and feeling. Validation, encouragement, and assistance come from the God within, the loving wise self. But challenges by others can awaken an amazing potential to see a greater truth—one that lies beyond the familiar reality. In a relationship the pressure to fulfill your partner's personality desires may get so strong that your trust in your inner wisdom is challenged. This is an opportunity to reconnect with your Higher Self.

Occasionally you can be drawn into someone's energy field that seems heavy and dense. She may be polite, saying all the right things, but you suddenly feel depressed, or anxious, or fearful for no reason. If her negativity at that moment is stronger than your positive view of yourself, you may feel as if you have been hit with a brick. Your own negative feelings may seem out of all proportion. No one has consciously intended you any harm, but any stray, dense vibrations and resulting murky colors in one energy field can provide an entry point for similar vibrations in another.

If you get caught temporarily in yielding to other people's beliefs or demands instead of trusting in the authority of your own Higher Self, you may find yourself in a battle of personalities and experience an outburst of temper or a quieter but equally potent anger or hurt. See it as an older pattern heaving its last breath. Anger or resentment, guilt or rejection that has been pushed back is going to surface in the intense vibration of light that is pouring into your life now. Anyone who calls to the surface a part of your personality that has been lurking behind the scenes can help you expand.

Your clear energy field reveals to others their inner beauty.

At other times you can be pulled into another person's electromagnetic energy field which embraces you with a sense of compassionate love or a sense of peaceful bliss. If his field is equal to or lighter than yours you may see your inner beauty very clearly when you are with him. Even ordinary greetings ("hello, how are you, nice day") can evoke unconditional love and the delight in simply being alive. One man describes it as a feeling of being forgiven when he is in the energy field of such a person. This pervading sense of happiness is actually the combining of the fragrances of two Higher Selves.

The light of your radiant temple disperses fear.

As you spin Bridges of Light to soul qualities, you draw more light into your energy field, and an immediate friction can be set up between the new energy and old patterns which no longer are working for you. Your work in these times is to deal only with *your* fears. Fear is stimulated by clinging to any belief that is too limited and small for you now. As a child, everyone had moments of fearing a path at night, imagining that monsters were going to lurch out at him. Even the trees with their waving branches were suspect. As an adult moving toward a higher consciousness, everyone still has moments of fearing to move past what is familiar, especially when he can't *see* the light on his path.

Any part of your personality can be frightened by whatever is new and unexplored. It can give endless rational reasons to retrench and stay on the familiar path of beliefs—even limited beliefs about yourself. These beliefs might be that you are capable of making a living only if you work for someone else, that you are not valuable to the world, or that you are not innately loving and wise. But all fears can change in the light of your temple.

If someone comes to you who is fearful or angry, you can let that astral energy pass over you without fearing or fighting it. The fears in anyone else need not affect you. The radiant light of your temple causes them to simply bounce away from your own energy field. By simply imagining yourself in the temple you are there and are protected, not only from outside patterns of fear, but from any negative energies that cross your path.

LAUNA *It's easy to see how fears of making a mistake can stop people from moving into what they see as their true purpose. Tom, a 48-year-old attorney in one of my workshops, described himself as straddling two boats, one foot in each. He was very interested in living from a higher consciousness, but the longer he put off a firm commitment, the wider apart the boats seemed to float, and the greater the leap needed to plant both feet squarely in the one boat. He recog-*

nized an old pattern of fear that he would make a mistake! But this time he was determined to deal with it from a new point of trust. He built a Bridge of Light to the core energy of trust every night and every morning for ten days. While driving to and from work he said the word "trust" aloud, observed the thoughts that came to him, and said it again, each time more intrigued with the thoughts that followed its energy. Only then did he begin to gain the confidence that he could step into the boat that was marked with his true purpose instead of holding on to the one that was taking him where he was hoping to make the most money, but which depleted his energy. With this confidence he began to plan his next step. This man is now actively using his skills to mediate with divorcing couples so that the children involved will be supported by the love of both parents. He loves his work and he is using all of his skills and training at the same time.

Peter, a 45-year-old president of a family business, used the Bridge of Light to trust for several months before he decided to change his business from one which was concerned only with profit to one which shared decisions and profits with the workers. He did this despite a lingering fear that he might be making a mistake. The next year the profits were up. The employees were enthusiastic, loyal, contented, and healthy. They loved taking more responsibility. Many began new educational programs. Peter is delighted with his company now, and even his conservative father who founded the business has begun to support his changes.

JAIWA Fears of making mistakes are there to remind you to take that pattern of fear into the light before making a decision. From our viewpoint, mistakes don't happen. Whatever you look back on as a mistake was actually an opportunity to develop certain skills that you needed. They might be practical skills that are learned from the outside world or inner skills of patience, perseverance, or joy. Only when you look back and imagine that another choice would have been better does the one you made seem like a mistake.

Some people are afraid they will have hard lessons to learn if they make a mistake. But lessons do not necessarily impose a negative experience. In school there is a math lesson, a language lesson, an art lesson—and only the fear of not doing well makes one dread those lessons. Self-judgment sets the tone of any lesson. If someone feels that she is doing a wonderful job considering her lack of experience and the challenge at hand, all learning can be exhilarating.

The fear of making a mistake and not succeeding can prevent success temporarily, but not for long when your intention to succeed is stronger than the fear. As soon as the fear loosens its hold, you will see obvious ways to go about bringing your vision into reality. Every time a fearful reaction comes up, there is an opportunity to permeate it with the light of trust. Add a bridge to confidence and clarity for an even more solid base of support.

Imagine that your fear was there to remind you that some idea or belief is no longer working for you and that releasing any attachment to the old opens the door to reach the new. Whatever you have put off doing for several days or weeks may well be blocked by a hidden fear. For example, fear is frequently behind procrastination—such as reading the newspaper from front to back every morning instead of spending some time in your temple before going to work. An unconscious fear of opening to too much light may be operating if you compulsively read about events which have little meaning to you.

Dissolving fear clears your intuitive knowing.

Sometimes when you tune in to your intuition, it is difficult to tell what is intuition and what is a move to avoid risk or fear. Hidden fears of making a mistake often seem like intuition, while the real intuition is being blocked by the fear. The more important and serious you consider the action you are about to take, the more fear may be generated. For example, several people, thinking their intuition was giving them warning of an earthquake, sold their homes and moved to small towns fifteen years ago. The big earthquake didn't happen, and looking back, one of this group said that he was simply motivated by fear.

You can always recognize an intuitive knowing because it is a moment of direct knowing and bypasses the emotions. The longer you can hold a connection to your Higher Self without any emotional reaction, the more clear and direct the knowledge you receive will be. As a result of the contact, feelings of joy, anticipation, satisfaction, and peace often emerge. These are the emotions to watch for when you are discerning what information came from intuition.

Face fears by tuning to your intuitive knowledge.

You can tune to intuitive knowing beyond the rational mind when you are facing a fear. Bring the fear into the open, and look at it clearly. This step alone will dissipate much of its hold. If there are two jobs open, both in the field you desire, and it is very important that you take the one in which you would be most effective, how would you make the choice? After considering the people you would be working with, their expectations, your own abilities, and your own creative desires, what next?

Your decision will be much clearer if you uncover any fears you have by asking yourself what is the worst possible thing that could happen if you make the choice you are afraid of. If you look at choices this way, fears can surface and be handled by your rational mind. Fears are nearly always irrational, and quickly subside once your rational mind has the opportunity to deal with them. They belong to the emotional plane, and your rational mind can act as a kindly parent to many fearful feelings. Your intellect can take account of all the possibilities and potentials before offering you the most likely outcome for both jobs.

Your intuitive knowing can reach you in your Temple of Light. Fears tend to hang around outside the door of the temple, reluctant to enter such a glowing, radiant place. Once inside, you can tune your spiritual antennae to "intuition" and sense which job offer stands in the greater light when you sense it. Intuition works through symbols rather than words, and one picture can give you more information than a thousand words.

You can live by the authority of your own soul.

If you want to live from confidence and enthusiasm instead of fear, you can do it by the authority of your own soul. Trust is the first step. It is also the second step, and the last step. Trust is every step. As you increase your trust in the unlimited power and light of your own formless essence, you will find it possible to actually live from the wisdom of a new reality.

With trust, a brief storm of mass fear or panic cannot penetrate your energy field. There may be times ahead when you need to take refuge in your temple until a wave of fear created by mass anxiety passes over you. Panic will rise in waves if people are stirred by mass thought forms of fear. We see these waves hitting people and watch them veer off course, as a flock of birds veers when the lead bird decides there is danger ahead. This is a time when you cannot trust your leaders to remain free from these surges of fear. You can only trust your own soul from the stillness of your temple. We guides do not see any big catastrophes looming on the horizon. Neither catastrophic world wars nor economic collapse are destined to happen to your planet. It is only the mass fear that can create these. It permeates the energy of light with dark, cloudy colors and causes a dissonant and disturbing vibration. Trust adds a bright electric blue to your energy field and enhances its resonance as it reverberates throughout the universe. Trust is a powerful force that rebalances whatever it is focused upon.

If you should get caught in a crosscurrent of fear or panic, remember that many great intelligences and beings of light from outside this planetary system are focusing light upon the earth at this pivotal point of human transformation. When you turn your eyes inward and upward and open your heart to receive, you know you are always protected by your Higher Self. Simply shake off any residue from your aura, as a shaggy dog shakes water from its coat. Then rinse your aura with a shower of light.

EXERCISE
A SHOWER OF LIGHT

When to use it: You can bathe yourself in an abundant shower of light when any self doubts arise, or when fatigue or a physical illness threatens. Any imbalance in the body, emotions, or mind sends a signal to the brain. If you heed the signal, you can restore inner harmony and trust very quickly.

What does it do? A shower of light does for the psychic body what a shower of fresh water does for the physical body. It washes away the dust and grime of frustrations that have crossed your energy field. After a day out in the world where you are in contact with psychic turmoil, rinsing your psyche off with a shower of light restores and rejuvenates your energy. It prevents the lodging of denser material in your aura.

How long does it take? About ten minutes or less.

Process: Imagine a ray of light above your head that forms a spray of light, like a shower. Imagine droplets of light falling all over your body and about three feet around it. See the drops in different colors. The color you focus on will be the most predominant. If you want more energy, focus on red. If you need a stronger calming trust, use blue. If you desire healing, create an abundance of green. If you are preparing to enter your Temple of Light or to create Bridges of Light, shower your psyche with violet drops of light. There are abundant showers of light available in every color. Imagine the healing droplets flowing over and through your body. Continue until you feel squeaky clean through and through.

EXERCISE
TUNNEL OF LIGHT

JAIWA Imagine that you are in a tunnel with walls made of luminous light. You are floating through it, your body spinning slowly so that you lose any sense of which way is up, down, right, or left. Imagine swirling through this tunnel surrounded by colors that are bright and pure. See the reds, roses, greens, pinks, golds, turquoises, blues, greens, and violets. Imagine that these brilliant colors are literally dissolving any negative energy and freeing you to feel balanced and joyful again.

Each time you do this exercise, bring in the colors that are the most intensely pleasurable. Let your weightless body turn as it moves through the tunnel of colors. This is a very healing exercise for the mind as well as the emotions. As you become skillful at visualizing the colors of the rainbow in your tunnel of light, the effect increases. Your body will feel different when you come out of the tunnel—relaxed and revitalized from the healing power of each color radiating through your body.

LAUNA *Another very real challenge—how do we handle the feeling of being out of control when we face a crisis? What tools will help us to handle unexpected emergencies in our lives? How can we see a challenge approaching and change the situation before a problem or crisis arises?*

JAIWA

Each experience has a seed of wisdom within it for you.

You can meet every situation as a chance to weave another layer of light into your life. When you bring light into an experience, you alter your future. First, identify one or two skills that you most wish to learn. It may be to speak out honestly, to feel in control of your life, or how to connect with new friends. Keeping that wish in mind, you may begin to notice how each experience is teaching you what you have wanted to master. If you want new friends, your Higher Self may provide you with opportunities to improve your skills in relating with some of the friends you have now before you meet the new friends. Or you may be learning from each experience how to speak out honestly. Consider the experiences where you hesitated to speak as a rehearsal for the next time when you will be prepared to say what you wish.

If an experience lasts a long time, you may be learning many skills and expanding several higher qualities. You can speed your movement through any situation that you don't want by building a Bridge of Light from the situation to the qualities of understanding and loving compassion. The combination of these qualities alters the original situation, and usually in ways you won't expect.

What challenged you last year probably seems easy to handle now. What challenges you today will seem easy to handle next month, and by next year it is unlikely that you will be distracted by that type of challenge at all. Your ease comes from the experience of going through the doubt and uncertainty, or the fear and anxiety that happens when a challenge comes up that seems bigger than your resources are. This is what happens when you feel out of control; you are facing a new situation which requires greater resources of knowledge or compassion, and you can handle it by drawing in extra resources of light.

A true crisis offers an explosive energy to break into a free and open space.

At some time everyone has been challenged with a crisis. It might have been a crisis of physical health, of emotional trauma, or a mental clash of beliefs. Facing such a crisis can give you a new perspective on your life.

The faster that someone is expanding, the more *potential* crises are handled on the way. If no changes are made in thinking or lifestyle, one can sometimes coast along for years. A potential crisis is very different from a full-blown one. The farther ahead you can see it building up, the less effort is involved in handling it. For example, if a man wants to change his job and work in a business that he really believes in, he learns other skills, makes connections, and prepares a new way, perhaps with an interim job to help him make a transition.

A few years ago, the big jolts that shook a person to the core came only rarely. They were like an inner earthquake. But once they were over people relaxed and expected to be able to live peacefully again for a few years. Now as the waves of intense energy come in, these jolts are more frequent.

Almost all crises are agreed upon in some part of the unconscious mind *before they happen*. Often there is a dream that foretells what could happen if a certain direction is followed. Or one has a moment of sensing a crisis looming in a relationship, an investment, or a job—and decides to ignore the warnings. Talk to others who are in the midst of handling a crisis in their marriage, profession, or family life, and almost every time they will tell you that they "had a feeling something like this was going to happen." The crisis is to create a breakthrough in some place where they were caught in an unproductive situation. To handle it, people often reevaluate their lives and beliefs and then take some action that is new to them. They say or do things that show an inner strength they didn't know they had.

You have a special warning device within to tell you before a challenge or crisis is building.

A friend who had a very heavy brass bell hanging in her study got a feeling one night that she should raise the bell higher so it would be out of reach of people's heads who came in the room. My friend intended to move the bell the very next morning, but before she had done so, she absentmindedly walked into the room herself and straight into the big brass bell. Not only did she move the bell, but now at the first hint of a problem she needs to handle, she sees that big brass bell in her mind and decides to take action now *before* there is a problem.

Physical crises of health or accidents are there to quickly bring one's life into a new level of harmony.

Most people's lives have been endangered many times whether they consciously realized it or not. In a crisis of a life in danger people call for help immediately from their God within or God without. The person drops all attention to personality solutions. The correct action is sensed as an instant knowing—and action is taken. This is wisdom in action. Even though the personality may shriek in fear, and there is an awareness of the mounting terror from different sides of oneself, it is possible to hear and respond to a higher wisdom. People who escape death in an automobile accident or near-drowning incident recall clearly how time seemed to stop and they had abundant time to know what to do. Because the consciousness of the Higher Self works outside of the sense of time, an amazing level of information can be given in a split second of clock time. Were all this information coming through the rational side of the mind, it would take several hours to absorb it and make the calculations necessary for action. After the crisis is handled, you may notice a much deeper sense of peacefulness and harmony. Each life-death crisis brings in a soul quality that then becomes a part of your energy field.

Emotional crises clear the air for true joy.

Every emotional pain that you experience—from hurt to anger or guilt—calls attention to a part of the personality that is asking for an even stronger connection to the light. Sometimes crying helps to release the inside emotional pressure. At other times it helps even more to laugh. Emotional pain can be transformed by going into your place of healing love in your temple and basking in its healing energies. You can absorb enough photons of love in this room to rebalance each emotion and bring a positive flow of good feeling.

If your feelings are pushed back and you feel the pressure building into a depression, spin a Bridge of Light to the soul quality of humor. After you are standing on the bridge to humor, ask if there *were* an outrageous way of feeling good right now, what it would be?

Rather than comb through the cause of emotions you don't want, we suggest that you deliberately choose an activity that allows you to experience the emotions you do enjoy. For example, you can contact several people who are important to you and tell them so. Or call someone and tell him how much you appreciate who he is. Such activities release you from a wave of negative energy that has washed over you so that you can ride the waves of positive energies that are rolling in so powerfully now.

A Bridge of Light to wisdom and clarity illumines your mind to handle mental crises.

A mental crisis is a clash of two strong beliefs that are in direct opposition to each other. As you begin to integrate your new insights and understandings from the temple, old beliefs may conflict with new ones. For example, you might believe that your life will not be complete unless you have children and yet you are very involved in a career you have developed which you enjoy. You may believe that your money should be used to support the new global changes and yet also believe that you should save it for possible needs of your own at a later date. Or you may believe that marriage should last forever and yet realize that your relationship is having a destructive effect on both of you. These are crises which require you to bring a greater light to your mind, for it is your illumined mind which is able to project into the future and see the most probable outcome of your decision. It is the illumined mind which can see with such clarity that it can make a decision based upon a higher truth, and handle any fears with ease. You can bring that illumination to your mind by calling in a Bridge of Light to clarity and to wisdom. The energy of these two soul qualities will fill your mind with the insights and the understanding that it needs when such challenges and crises arise.

When two strong beliefs within you seem to oppose each other, it is your illumined mind that can often construct a third way of looking at the situation and bring the two beliefs together into a united whole.

When a soul crisis is faced, a new consciousness is born.

The greatest crises are those involving the soul. These are the spiritual crises—the times when you are faced with taking action on a commitment to the soul. These crises may last for months or years as you reflect deeply and make a choice that will affect the rest of your life. Often people are asking on such a deep level for more light that *every* situation is an answer to that request. They may face crises in several areas of life at once. Yet the underlying cause may be a soul crisis.

A person emerges from a soul crisis as if from a new life. Sometimes it feels as if some commitment made long ago is only now coming to light to be remembered and acted upon. It nearly always involves greater responsibility, to oneself or to a larger group. It may seem as if a crisis of this kind is being caused by some situation over which you have no control—that the world is doing it to you. But these crises only happen when one has made the inner commitment to see them through, to handle whatever is standing in the way of a much fuller life of expression and awareness. The crisis is there to clear every obstruction to true self-fulfillment. Illusions that confused the thinking are cleared, and behold, a new life becomes possible.

A spiritual crisis draws you closer to your Higher Self and guides.

If you could see yourself as we guides see you, you would be amazed at how far you have come in so short a time. Your courage to open to the reality of the soul's wisdom, even though it may not yet be recognized by some people, makes a dramatic change in your field of energy. You begin to draw in pure colors that give you a new clarity alongside the courage. With clarity and courage in your field of energy, you can face whatever comes up in your life.

What to do if you are facing a crisis.

If you have a friend to talk with who is wise and loving, someone who knows how to listen and to help you hold a focus on the real issues that you are working with, use that friend.

Make a contact with the metaphysical center in your town if there is one. Even if there isn't a permanent location for one, there are many groups forming now and meeting in homes. These groups often bring in experienced transpersonal speakers and workshop leaders. These centers are founded by light workers. They have connections with other people like you in your community. They are a direct route to connecting with groups or individuals who are facing the same spiritual crises that you are now facing. Your metaphysical bookstore owner or manager usually knows of these groups or can connect you with the people who have some experience in spiritual crises. Often a book may offer answers you need. Become sensitive to the books that carry light as well as words.

Spin a Bridge of Light to the quality of clarity, and gradually bring about the circumstances that match your vision, such as a home environment that is attractive and peaceful, a meaningful and pleasant work situation, or a relationship that truly nourishes you.

Go to your telepathic room of sending and receiving in your temple. In that room imagine thousands of people reaching out to you from the soul level, offering you all that they have and all that they know. Feel the strength of the group. Even though you have no physical contact with them, the soul contact is immediate and direct. You can feel an immediate lift of spirit. There will always be many people who are distributing the light and love they have gathered in meditation to other light workers.

You can make this inner connection every day. Large numbers of people are connecting soul to soul to send energy to each other. The key to the transformation of consciousness is through creating a Bridge of Light among all of you. See the power of the gridwork that you can form this way and thus tap into the pool of knowledge created by the minds and experience of each individual. You are part of this group and you are needed.

When you connect soul to soul telepathically with the light workers around the planet, there is an immediate sweep of energies through your heart center as well as through the higher mind. You feel healed and rebalanced, supported and loved. In that womb of deep knowing and receiving this love, you can see the true issues before you and understand what is needed. You know that you do not have to face anything alone.

Fortunately, the Higher Self always responds when asked for greater light to understand what is happening. When the emotions are calm and the mind slows down, understanding follows. The practical steps that you take after deep reflection about a life direction happen after you have made a commitment from deep within, even though you may not consciously realize it at the time.

As a result of crises you gain a gentler spirit of understanding, compassion, or humility. These gradually become a part of your natural response no matter what happens. No one else can judge which decision is the right one or the "spiritual" one and which is not. The knowledge can only come from the Higher Self of the person in crisis.

LAUNA *A friend who was making one of these lifetime decisions described herself as not having any solid ground to stand on. With her personal lifestyle uprooted, no visible way to earn a living, her marriage falling apart, and debts mounting, she felt shaky about what she would do or how she would manage her life. She stopped and looked at her life and the direction it was going in. She was almost 40 years old and afraid to take a clear stand. Suddenly she realized that the only thing that had any true value to her was the reality of her own guide and her Higher Self. After deep reflection and communication with her guide she made a clear commitment to use all of her energy and her time to serve this higher intelligence who had such a compassionate nature. She worked very long hours, doing what she did best, teaching seminars and writing books. In three years she had paid off all of her debts from credit cards and loans, bought a new car, handled her divorce with grace, and was bringing in enough income to support herself by doing the work she loved. She turned a point of crisis into a lifetime commitment without any outside assurance that it*

would work, and she achieved a triumph of success on every
level.

When I was writing my first book, Connecting With All
the People in Your Life, I would sit down with each chapter
and ask for higher guidance, but I could not understand why
one crisis after another was happening in my personal life
when I was trying to put all of my attention and time on the
book. It took me three years of writing full-time to complete
the book, and almost that long to realize that every crisis was
a response by my own soul to give me "higher guidance." By
going through each experience I was writing about, I was
challenged to actually live everything I wrote. My soul saw to
it that I learned the lessons well—so well that the new responses began to seem natural. Tremendous light poured into
my life, which greatly empowered the book, but more than
once left my personality feeling like an avalanche had hit it.
The result is a guidebook that is affecting many lives as
people identify a heart pattern to replace the belief or feeling
that isn't working—before a crisis arises. In my personal life
there are no more avalanches—just very loving friends who
amaze me with their expanding radiance.

If we listen carefully, we may catch ourselves setting up a
new challenge or crisis with a seemingly casual statement to
ourselves. One man was determined to make his marriage work,
and after great trials he said to himself that he would make it
work if it was the last thing he ever did. Three years later he and
his wife agreed upon an amicable divorce, and he soon discovered that he had the beginnings of a terminal illness. According
to his doctor, had he not made some change that restored his
sense of value and purpose he would have been seriously ill
within the next few months.

We can all learn to catch problems early and handle them
long before anyone is hurt or angered; or in the case of fi-
nances, we can see a probability before we run out of money

and set up a way to earn more. A woman who has grown tremendously in six months said, "I have this strange sense of urgency that every minute counts. I want to go through every challenge as rapidly as I can, and learn more with every experience. But I am scared to death that I am expanding so fast I will leave my husband behind. Part of me is trying to hold back and the other part is urging me on." The challenge she was facing could escalate into a spiritual crisis, and she recognized it. Yet she was handling the problems now before a crisis developed. After a session together both she and her husband realized that his growth was unfolding one way and hers was unfolding another way. They had different needs and different goals, but they realized the validity of each other's growth and chose to honor it. Today they are both expressing a very warm acceptance of each other's needs and offering their love in new ways to each other.

J A I W A

Every crisis opens the space for a richer life.

Each crisis reflects some area of life that is being healed or awakened. Looking back, it is easier to realize the gain. If the value of a crisis is not clear, ask, and insights may come quickly. Often the loss of money or a job, even the loss of a relationship, offers a desired level of freedom and self-awareness that wasn't there before. Any loss is there to create the space for a much more fulfilling life than what was lost.

Every crisis teaches how to discriminate what has real substance from what only appears to be solid. The earth looked flat for most of humanity's history, but the flatness was the illusion of a very limited view. Many current beliefs may soon be revealed to be as illusory as the flat earth belief. Use humor when you see them; letting go can be much easier.

Beliefs that are left over from youth can also be shaken loose, such as feeling inferior, discouraged, or unworthy. Ask your Higher Self to assist, and imagine that a space is being cleared on the landing field around you, so that creative ideas can make a smooth landing. Thoughts may start flowing to you in the middle of the day or the middle of the night, when you least expect them. They may be practical ones, such as a new place to live, or finding a group of people you enjoy who are on a similar path of discovery as yours.

If your mind should start going in circles without really getting anywhere when you are trying to make an important decision, give it a well-deserved rest. Cleaning out the garage or weeding the garden may seem like a funny opening for the understanding you are looking for, but often the best ideas can come through when the body is engaged and the mind is at ease. Try using everything as a metaphor. Throw away a half-empty can of old paint from the garage, and feel your spirit lift as if you are throwing away an old belief that doesn't enrich your life. Or pull up an overgrown weed and feel the relief as you lift it out roots and all.

Handling crises and challenges can be intense, but also quite exciting and exhilarating—a bit like paddling a kayak. The first thing one learns is how to roll the kayak. The kayaker purposely turns it over and then rolls it around until it turns upright again, while she remains seated in it. Once she masters the rollover recovery in a calm lake, she knows how to handle it in the big waves.

If you should lose your temper, become irritable with your mate, impatient with your child, or resentful toward your boss, think of it as a rollover to practice bringing yourself upright again. Even though you may still be in the middle of white water as your balance is regained, you can simply fasten your eyes on where you are going and paddle vigorously until the water is calm again and you can relax.

Every person has a spiritual mission here, and many are going through confusion and doubt. You can help them by bringing them on to a Bridge of Light with you. It takes about one minute and can seem like a miraculous lift to their spirit—even when they have no idea that you are doing it. Each time you can imagine this light within another person, everyone is blessed. No matter how hard you try, you cannot bless others more profoundly than you are blessing yourself when you see them as beings of light clothed in a colorful personality.

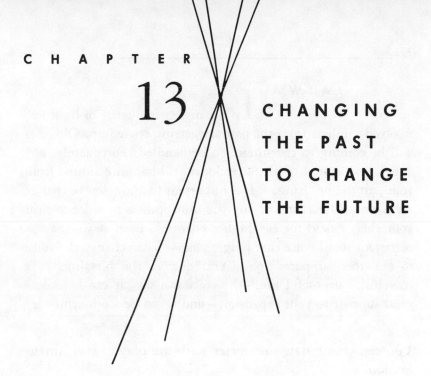

C H A P T E R

13

CHANGING
THE PAST
TO CHANGE
THE FUTURE

LAUNA "If only I could go back and change my past mistakes," clients tell me. As they open to the light, they see mistakes they made before their vision became more clear. Some even feel that years of their lives have been wasted while they pursued something which now has no meaning to them.

We all want to change something about our past—but few of us realize we can begin again by clearing out all guilts and regrets that have blocked our enthusiastic embrace of abundant love and wisdom. We can do it by changing our memories of an experience and building in a good memory.

JAIWA

In the higher frequency of light unresolved conflicts from the past are getting stirred up. Old fears will be coming to the surface to be handled. Fortunately, any anger, resentment, guilt, or jealousy still hanging around from your past can be changed. It is important to know *how* to change the memories that are causing you unhappiness in order to clear your energy field for the higher energies. Even if you have a persistent small voice that judges you, you can change the voice to one that supports you. "You deserve the blessings of a powerful, purposeful life," the voice can say. It can become a great support to your expansion—and it can be a powerful one.

You can create new memories with the play of your imagination.

You can tap into a tremendous power for creating a positive, purposeful life by using a Bridge of Light to remove old memories and establish new ones that will radiate abundance into your future. This power comes from your direct recognition of your own divinity as a creator. You decide what kind of memory you want to create, and proceed to build it into your memory bank as real.

By consciously changing memories of the past, you free the energy that was holding each negative memory together. Now you can use this free energy for fulfilling your highest possible future. The process activates your imagination so that a new future can unfold like a rich tapestry. We guides call it high play, but if you look closely it is purposeful play. The fundamental truth behind this kind of play is profound: You can set up the future you want when you know how to change your past. All anyone really has of a past experience is a memory. Who is to say that you have not already changed what actually happened with your selective memory—leaving out certain parts, emphasizing and exaggerating others?

Until the wisdom inherent in any experience is truly understood it can be prudent to hold onto the memory—just as one would guard a heavy chest that contained a treasure until the key could be found to open it and get the treasure out. By uncovering the knowledge gained from every experience, you can free the energy that has kept the memory in place. And every bit of energy that you free from the past contributes to your power to do whatever has the greatest value to you now.

Each of you has several potential futures already forming.

One of these futures is the most likely to happen. Its probability is determined by the image that you now have of who you are—your memories of successes, failures, attributes, strengths, and weaknesses. To change this image of yourself, you can relive a past experience through the new lens of what could have happened if greater wisdom, compassion, or understanding had been available.

The process to loosen a memory and create a new one is very simple. We guides have found that the glue that holds your memories in place is light-soluble. Just as water-soluble glue dissolves when water is applied, memory-holding glue dissolves when light is applied. By connecting a Bridge of Light directly into a memory, you can illuminate the negative memory pattern and dissolve it. Next, you can replace it with a new experience which feeds the subconscious mind with powerful, positive memories. Thus, your most probable future is lightened and expanded.

Since the subconscious mind does not make a distinction between an actual experience and an imagined one, you are erasing a negative picture and replacing it with a new one. You have done this many times—relived and reinterpreted or selectively remembered only the part of an event that enriched and empowered you. This skill in memory selection helped get you where you are now, but you may not have realized the wisdom in the process.

When you create a memory of being wise and loving, your life becomes more flexible and open.

When you change a memory, your life immediately shifts to accommodate this new reality and your sense of self becomes stronger. What used to seem like the *only* choice can open to new choices. Automatic reactions to someone else— trying too hard to please or ignoring someone's needs—can open to new responses. Reactions in which you could not see another viewpoint and resisted change can dissolve. Where you said yes, you may now say no without apology or stress. Where you said no to yourself or to others, you may now say yes—and mean it.

LAUNA *There may be many things about the past that we would like to change now as we look back. The choices we made before we began working so closely with the Higher Self may need to be expanded, changed, or adjusted in some way to be in harmony with our awareness now. Rather than look back with regret or guilt on something we did or a bad choice we made, we can ask ourselves if we consciously thought of a better choice and decided to take the second-best choice. Considering all of our experiences, our hopes and fears, our beliefs and goals, we always make the best decision available to us at each moment. Now we have so much light coming into our lives that we can see a wiser choice. Once we can acknowl-*

edge that we did the best we could we are ready to release the memory and build in a new one in its place that matches the light in our lives now.

A therapist in Dallas, Jean St. Martin, specializes in creating new memories of the past in order to create a new future. With the precision of an accomplished therapist who works with light, Jean helps her clients to look at what could have happened if their Higher Selves had been in charge. They gradually build a new memory, detail by detail, acting as if it is happening now with a new dialogue and outcome until the new experience registers as real and the bad feelings are replaced with lightness.

One of her clients, a 16-year-old boy, was terribly unhappy with himself. He felt he had made one mistake after another and was never going to amount to anything. Jean helped him to imagine his past differently, to see how each experience had added to his life and served him. Then she helped him to build in new and positive memories of his past. Within a few sessions he was becoming cheerful and optimistic about himself and his future. What amazed him was suddenly recalling numerous positive experiences from his past that had really happened! The former negative memories had buried them. Somehow the newly installed happy experiences of the past had triggered the other good ones to come to the surface. Today he is the leader in a choral group at school and loves teaching his friends how to "change" their past. Jean says the wonder of releasing past memories of unhappiness is that the future shifts so rapidly to fit the newly created "past."

The following process is very powerful. Plan to allow some undisturbed time. If you choose to do it, you may be able to create important shifts in your life.

TOOL OF LIGHT
CHANGING UNPLEASANT MEMORIES TO
NEW AND PLEASANT ONES

Begin by breathing slowly and deeply, once again going through your meadow, up the mountain and into your Temple of Light. Go to the round room of healing love with the photons of love circling around in it. It has clear crystal and amethyst panels which allow the light filtering through to dissolve every toxic memory that has ever caused you pain.

For this exercise, choose an unpleasant memory from the past, a recent one, or one from ten or twenty years ago. On a scale of 1 to 10, choose a 5 or less until you are skilled in this way of using your creative imagination.

Think of several people who have profoundly influenced your life for the better. Connect with the Higher Self of each one and invite her or him to sit with you in this room. Seat this group in a circle and let them be a council of elders to assist you. Explain to them that you wish their support in releasing a guilt or negative memory (a hurt, loss, grief, or regret) from the past.

Tell them the memory you wish to change. Get a clear sense of how you hoped the situation you are describing would turn out, and also a sense of what you feared might happen. Tell this to your Council of Elders.

After you express the specific negative memory, pause and listen carefully to each response. Observe how sincerely each person wants you to have a wonderful life. As each one speaks to you of his or her unconditional love, the room may seem more radiant.

Allow your council of elders to offer you wisdom gained from their own experiences and wisdom. At least one of the members of this council will have had a very similar experience and be able to share an important piece of understanding for your process. Imagine how different your past experience would have been if you had had the wisdom and the love of this council of elders with you during the experience.

Create a movie of the outcome of the experience if your highest hopes had manifested into reality. Encircled by the group of elders in your temple, imagine they are helping you to create a new memory in which love and wisdom changed the outcome. (Don't expect to actually "see" the scene as you see when your eyes are open. You are working with an inner sight, much more subtle than physical sight, but as real and powerful.)

Now recall the first inkling you had that things might not work out as you had pictured, and ask yourself these questions: "What would have happened if I had known how to spin a Bridge of Light at this very point in this experience? What would I have said, and how would I have acted?"

Stop here and actually spin a Bridge of Light to this point in the memory. Use love or wisdom (or both) and permeate the experience with a brilliant light. Allow yourself to actually feel or to mentally sense this new understanding now as it flows into your body and mind—tingling, warming, and expanding.

Brighten the movie in your imagination and make it larger than life. See yourself reliving the memory from the first point of challenge as you relate from the heart, receiving ideas that weren't there before, excited about the possibilities of what can be done. Hear yourself speaking with honesty and wisdom.

You can also spin a Bridge of Light to other soul qualities which would have made a difference if you had known how to access them—compassion, clarity, and humor. Each has a different color and carries a specific vibration to change the experience of your past.

Now turn again to your council of elders and share with them the new memory. With your inner ear, listen to the resonance of each word as you speak to them from a new understanding.

For a few minutes simply experience in advance an enriched

sense of how much more is possible now. Imagine how it will be to live in this reality, consulting with this wise and loving group, seeing the fruits of your work, delighting in doing what you love.

Sitting in the center of this powerful circle of beloved friends from your own soul group, imagine your future as far out into the future as you wish. Get a sense of what you will be doing. How will you feel about yourself, your work and your life?

After some practice with penetrating your past with light, you may want to choose a more intense memory of the past that you would like to change. What was impossible before because of a belief system that the past is impenetrable is now possible.

You can alter memories of relationships and of yourself and build a memory in which you gave and received deep love and understanding in each one. You can also create memories of being organized, clear, and powerful in your work. The future that you are changing begins immediately. Watch for the difference in your confidence and your ability to know the next steps to take.

Sometimes the transformation happens instantaneously; the painful feeling that went with the memory of a mistake is simply gone after inundating it with light. At other times it is a more gradual process, as if the memory is being dissolved layer by layer. Notice now the level of confidence you feel and the lighter spirit. After touching a memory with the Bridge of Light and imaginatively living the new memory, you have made your highest possible future more available than ever.

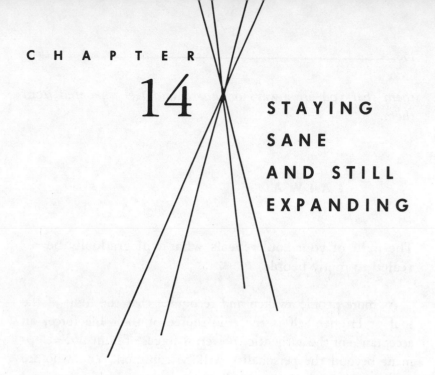

LAUNA *Spiritually awakening clients fre-*
quently ask me, "What is normal, anyway?" Am I still sane
even if some people I know think there is something wrong
with my personal philosophy of life now? Is it sane to be in the
majority and insane to be in the minority? How do I convince
my marriage partner that I am not going off the deep end, my
mother that my beliefs are not interfering with my work, and
my friends that I have a sound mind in spite of our different
viewpoints about life? As a matter of fact, how do I convince
myself that I am not going too far out?

Sometimes someone close to you may think you are off
the track, ungrounded, weird, or flaky. If friends or family
members are suspicious about your beliefs, and you feel un-
comfortable with them, you could feel so cautious around

them that you are always on guard and feel separated from them.

J A I W A

The light of your soul reveals what will gradually be revealed to many people.

As more people awaken and recognize that the light of the soul or Higher Self is the true source of their life force, an acceptance of the authentic, powerful stages of human development beyond the personality will be common. You who are reading this book are not likely to fit into the mold for normal in the eyes of the general public, since "normal" simply means the average. As you integrate the new frequencies of light, you are on the leading edge of consciousness rather than in the mass thinking, and there are growing numbers of you. Many more are poised to break through and sense how much of their realities they are creating and how much more is possible.

The process of enlightenment requires a well-integrated personality as a base for the Higher Self's guidance. The light flowing into your mind can stimulate any personality tendency, such as a sense of superiority or inferiority, or an emotion such as sadness, loneliness, grief, or anger. If a major adjustment is suddenly demanded of your personality you may feel you have lost your balance. These feelings can all be handled with the tools you are mastering in each chapter. The quicker you recognize them, the easier they are to handle. Be patient with your personality as it assimilates the light of new knowledge. Any knowledge that goes beyond popular beliefs can sometimes make you feel isolated, especially when there is no proof in the outer world and your friends have not had similar experiences. But none of these symptoms means that you have a mental or emotional problem. You are simply cleaning up your whole field of energy in an extremely accelerated manner, and you may not be getting much support in the process.

Your mind can be sound and still be questioned by your own marriage partner or family members. A great deal depends on how many changes the other people in your life think you want *them* to make. If you can accept them just as they are without the need for them to be interested in transpersonal awareness, you can ease your path. Remember that they may think spiritual awakening is dangerous, lumping it all together with some who claimed to be spiritual leaders but lacked both wisdom and love. If you can imagine how strong their anxiety may be, you can understand why they are too fearful to investigate any realities beyond the material world.

Speak truthfully to others, but share only what is appropriate. What will keep you sane is to be very truthful to yourself and not pretend to believe something that you don't. Be disarmingly honest to yourself, and you will feel a steady, strong sense of self rising from within.

Look for people who share your vision of prosperity and peace for the world.

Your delight in learning and expanding your sensitivity to a higher consciousness is shared by many people around the world. You will find them in every walk of life, from the most humble to the most exalted. They may lead quiet lives at home or be leaders in their fields. As the new waves of energy reach full force you are finding each other, in cities and small towns, from one continent to another, and you are offering a supportive atmosphere for your mutual expansion. We watch many of you already sharing with friends how to create your own happiness, how to meditate with light, how to tap into the wisdom encoded within the heart. Notice how soundly you experience your sanity when you are with people who share your vision of how much is possible.

Your personality is working very rapidly now to integrate the new circuits of reality. If other people seem to cause disruptions or confusion, recognize them as a valuable part of your expansion in consciousness. Every insight or new understanding must be played out—with your mother, husband, wife, child, boss. Your integration of a new response, your willingness to speak honestly, to listen, and to accept others are your challenges and your victories.

LAUNA

Being "normal" means to the average person that others feel and act like him. "Too far out" means more than one step past his beliefs and experiences. When something can't be measured by volume or weight, some people are likely to question it. Before jogging became popular and had its own shoes to prove it was a real sport, people who ran up the street at dawn were considered quite strange. Even today, every culture has some customs that would seem crazy to members of another culture.

If a man fears that his wife is "going off the deep end," for example, it can mean that she has interfered with his comfort zone of belief. To some people meditation sounds okay for relaxation, but not okay for inner guidance. When you find yourself facing opposition to your growth from someone because you are too far out, sit down and in a spirit of compassion listen to her fears about you. Afterward you can agree that given how she sees the situation, you can understand that she would feel concerned. If you speak with this understanding and then re-

main silent, without defending yourself or blaming her, you may find that she begins to look at your spiritual interests differently. You have compassionately responded to a part of her that is afraid, and your response may calm that part so well that her concern about you turns to a calmer acceptance of your path.

JAIWA The same compassionate understanding works for each part of yourself that questions your sanity or common sense. If one side thinks you should be more concerned about the mechanics of living, listen to it and agree that considering its viewpoint you can understand how it would feel afraid. The more accepting you can be, the less opposition you will face from within your own self.

Appreciate everyone in your life, for each person you know brings out a different side of you. With one person you may never be late. With another, you may be repeatedly late no matter how hard you try to be on time. With one friend you may feel wise and powerful. With a few acquaintances who are rigid in their beliefs, you may feel a little crazy. In each case you are responding to people's images as they strike a chord within you.

All of these people reflect something that is also in you. That is why relationships are such an opportunity to integrate the light into every thought and feeling. The trait you see may not be a negative one; you may be surprised to realize that the radiant, loving quality in your child or your mate is reflecting the same intensity of understanding love that is within you.

Notice what you love and what annoys you in others, and you can gain a greater insight into a part of yourself that is ready to be acknowledged. Your Higher Self can take all of these into account simultaneously and communicate sound and sensible advice to you. Trust it.

LAUNA What is there about the real world that makes it "real," except an agreement by a majority of people? Maurice Bucke asserts in Cosmic Consciousness that when the color blue began to be visible to the human eye, the first people who could see it were considered crazy. Later, when seeing blue became common to the majority of people, the only people who seemed strange were those who couldn't distinguish blue as a real color. They were considered color blind. But we won't have to wait 100 years to be in the majority. Change is happening so fast now that those who try to wait until others validate their move into higher guidance may end up at the tail end of human expansion and transformation. Either end is all right, but why try to delay the obvious while we wait for the world's approval?

As we move from one rung to another on the ladder of higher consciousness, we can get caught between rungs. None of the roles we were playing seem appropriate, yet we are unable to let go of certain expectations or needs, such as wanting to belong, or to fit in with the majority. We know we can't go backward and be happy, and we are not sure we can go forward and be happy either. But if we try to step back onto a path we have already completed, we are immediately discontented and restless.

At these times we need only recognize how much inner strength we really have. What counts is the ability to persevere with a stable will. When we are between rungs of the ladder we don't quite belong anywhere. But as we step up to the next rung we assume a new role in life. Each role is closer to the vibration of our Higher Self or God self and offers us a greater harmony and efficiency.

Sometimes when we act from a direct response to our intuition, some people may say we are crazy for doing what we do. A friend faced this dilemma when she was offered the opportunity to make a very large profit (and to become famous) through a national television production. When she tuned to her intuition, she didn't have a good feeling about the offer, even though the sponsors made it sound very tempting. She finally decided to say no. The sponsors thought she was crazy to turn it down and told her so, but she acted from the integrity of her inner knowing, and is enjoying true peace of mind while she goes about her real work. As it turned out, the deal would not have made a profit for her, but even had it proved financially lucrative, she made her decision without needing a reason. To some people, this is crazy. To her, it was an exercise in trusting her inner guidance, a step she was very grateful she took. Instead of the television shows, she created a thriving business of her own and had a wonderful time doing it. She watched lives change as she taught others and validated their courage until they could launch themselves in new careers of their own choice.

One client's intense interest in metaphysical knowledge disturbed her family so much that she agreed to take all the psychological tests available to reassure them that she was balanced and sane. She answered hundreds of questions, drew pictures, told stories, and projected meaning into inkblots with the psychologist for six hours. The results of all the tests showed that she was not only normal, but extraordinarily bright, creative, and well integrated mentally and emotionally. Everyone relaxed, and she continued to study and meditate—with an occasional wink and smile to remind her father that she was absolutely normal.

Some people open to an awareness that is so different from the world around them, including their own family, that they need some outside support. Dr. John Enright, an understanding psychologist, obliged such a man, whose boss was threatening to dismiss him, with a letter stating that he was "sane." His *boss read it, relaxed his fears, and soon promoted the man to a more responsible position. Ten years later the man was still carrying the faded letter in his billfold. Armed with the "proof" that he was sane, he could confidently explore deeper dimensions of reality and enjoy his life.*

With such a letter by an acknowledged authority—a psychologist, psychiatrist, minister, or priest—perhaps many people would feel more adventurous in their quest to grow and expand. Why not write this letter from your Higher Self to your personality self, assuring it of its sanity and acknowledging how hard it is working to resonate with the Higher Self's vision? After all, the only person likely to need convincing is yourself.

A technique for handling others' fears about your being normal when you are following your highest vision, living with purpose, or acting with new courage and insight is to imagine that each critic is an actor hired to act out (and exaggerate) a fear that is in you. This has happened to me many times over the years. The drama can involve several characters, or just a quick short scene. If I have been criticizing myself, someone comes along and does it much more dramatically than I could. Whether he criticizes himself or me, the lesson is the same. When someone else exaggerates something I have experienced ("I should be doing more and doing it faster," or "I should be happy every minute") I may reach out with compassion, but if the same feeling of self-criticism is still in my own mind, I see the ludicrous nature of such a statement, the absolute self-absorption—a giveaway of a subpersonality speaking—and I smile. What a gift to be freed from one more of the glamours of the little self.

When I am impatient with my imperfections, a more impatient person steps into my life and I see the amazing waste of energy involved in impatience. He may not know the gift he has given me, but I do. Once I clearly recognize the misguided thinking on my part that matches the one being acted out by another person, the drama is over almost immediately.

J A I W A

Many people are simply afraid to experience a fuller revelation of who they are at this time, and their fear is projected onto you as a concern about your sanity. When you realize how they are feeling, your own compassion and caring can come to the surface. Instead of feeling bad about any judgments they might have about your beliefs, you can simply send them a silent blessing and be on your way.

S E C T I O N IV

ASSEMBLING

YOUR

HIGHEST

POSSIBLE

FUTURE

In this last section you begin to create your most purposeful and joyous future by sensing new choices in every aspect of your life. You will be deliberately choosing by the authority of your own soul, aware and responsible for the results of these choices. The inner strength gained from freely choosing your life prepares you for getting very clear about your purpose so you can create practical ways to express it. You will then learn ways to strengthen and revitalize your physical body by working with your light body so that you can act on your purpose now. Next, you will learn ways to select the spiritual assistance for your continued expansion, identify your true teacher, and select the spiritual group that is right for you. In the last chapter you will retreat to a quiet space in nature where you align your total being with the forces of light. Here you will begin to sound your own silent note that announces how much light and love you have integrated and balanced in your life. It is this clear note that can telepathically reverberate in the hearts of many people with healing force as they respond to its clarity, power, and beauty.

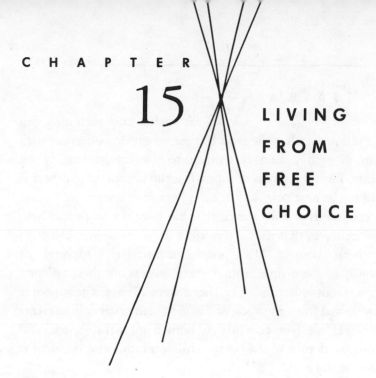

CHAPTER

15

LIVING FROM FREE CHOICE

LAUNA *S*ometimes we can become overwhelmed by the sheer quantity of choices and changes! Like the child who whispered to his teacher, "Do we have to do what we want to again today?" we are finding new choices available to us which weren't there before we opened to new light. How can we choose the path of the greatest light and expansion? With our beliefs changing so fast, how do we know the difference between acting responsibly and being mired in pointless obligations? If we are facing changing a job, a relationship, or city where we live, how do we make that choice wisely and then live with the results?

J A I W A

What makes this incoming period so unique is that the new higher vibrations offer as much freedom as each person is willing to take responsibility for handling. The old system of following the authority of others is phasing out as new points of light appear in every area of living.

For thousands of years the culture has taught that people have little free choice, that they are victims of circumstance and can't do anything about it. Most people automatically adopted the philosophy of the people around them, accepting these cultural beliefs without question. Yet there were always a few people who awakened from the spell of "victim" superstitions to create empires, explore new continents, launch men into space, and dive into the depths of the ocean while everyone else declared it couldn't be done.

In the new intensity of light, each of you can explore your own continents within the vast panorama of higher consciousness, launch yourself into the interstellar space of awareness, and dive into the depths of new understanding.

The most basic freedom on this planet is choosing the personal philosophy from which you live.

The choice of a personal philosophy determines all your other choices. It takes in all of your beliefs about life and death, the meaning and purpose of life, and what you truly value the most. Until now, people could drift along without much thought about their deeper beliefs. The deeper beliefs were always there, but they were underground, out of most people's awareness. People rarely changed their basic beliefs about their lives. Once you have opened to new light you have probably already discovered that your whole philosophy of life is changing rapidly. Light is synonymous with change. Just as the energy of the universe is always changing and moving, creating one form and then another in its play, your life will reflect changing forms as well.

We guides watch where people put their time and energy, not what they say, in order to ascertain their deep beliefs about life. Often we find someone who is living out a personal philosophy of joyful sharing of what he has—knowledge, talent, experience, love, and joy. He may not be able to put his philosophy into words, but clearly he has made his choices from his deep beliefs.

Acting responsibly is choosing from your highest wisdom.

You may sometimes feel confused between what is your responsibility and what you are doing out of a sense of obligation. If you keep commitments that are in line with your understanding of your life's highest purpose, you are acting responsibly. Obligation implies a burden, something that has been imposed from the outside, and responsibility comes from a commitment that you have freely chosen from the wisdom of your heart.

There's one sure way to tell the difference between obligations and true responsibility. Obligation continually feels like a burden. If you feel obligated, dutiful, or have slid into something without checking your intuitive knowing, it may feel like a burden. Where you have submitted to what someone else thought you should do, old patterns of feeling like a victim could come up. It's easy to feel passive or helpless in the face of difficulty when it seems that the project or relationship was someone else's idea. On the other hand, handling responsibility feels like a privilege and a delight. You may be working harder than ever, but you will be doing what you do because you absolutely believe in it. When your energy, time, and money all go where your heart is, you are freely choosing your life.

You will always know which jobs, relationships, and homes

you have chosen from your essence wisdom because if they temporarily turn into hard work, you won't mind the extra push. Once any decision is made from the heart, there is an abundance of energy available to carry it through.

Once you have determined your true responsibilities, you can use your energy to experiment with your highest visions and put your whole self into a new job, a new city, a new marriage, the decision to have a baby or be a loving parent. If you are challenged by problems to carry through with the changes you have chosen, and start blaming yourself for mistakes, remember how it felt as a child to learn to ride a bicycle—by focusing on the balance that kept you moving forward. Children are so delighted to keep their balance on a new bicycle for five or ten minutes that they forget about the crashes—and they become experts very quickly. Living from free choice is like learning to ride a bicycle. Focus on what *is* working, and you can expect delightful surprises when you are learning how to handle greater responsibility as a result of your choice for more light.

A good preparation when you are thinking of changing jobs, relationships, or cities is to first consider all of your choices. Note which ones tend to energize you when you think of them and which ones drop your energy. If the choice feels light or seems to have a special shimmer around it, this choice has a good chance for the success you are visualizing.

You don't always have to leave an unsatisfying situation to exercise your free choice. If you feel yourself to be trapped in a business or a job, ask yourself this question even if you don't think there is an answer: "If there *were* a way to make this job into one I would enjoy, what would it be?" Often you can make new arrangements that work for each person, especially when you know you have a choice of staying or leaving. The same is true of a relationship. If you feel guilty and unhappy every time you are with the other person, for example, you could be motivated to make a change in how you relate to each other—or you could ask the same question and see what ideas come to mind. Choosing light means finding the highest, lightest way to relate to everything in life—jobs, friends, and family.

As you consciously choose the reality by which to view your life and the world about you, think about the beliefs that will offer joyful expansion and growth. For example, what are the beliefs that will give you high energy and make it easier to share your own work with others? It is possible to look at your life as a struggle to learn, to understand, and to be happy, or to look at the very same life as one in which an incredible number of blessings have been and are still being showered upon you. The circumstances can be exactly the same, and two opposite viewpoints can be seen as equally true. It depends on the thinker's choice of interpretations.

By taking the stance that you are being accelerated in your growth by each change—whether you initiate it or it seems to be happening to you beyond your control—you will indeed make that belief a reality. Two people may have the same changes happening to them, in their marriages, their jobs, or their financial base. One feels shaken, resentful, and keeps replaying how he or she can get the old circumstances back again, while the other one focuses on the new opportunities presented. Even if a little fearful, the second person feels like a pioneer, confident that his Higher Self or his guide will lead him into the right circumstances and to the right people.

With your mind receiving more illumination and learning to hold steady in that light, you can identify beliefs that have caused unhappiness or apathy. It is possible to experience being trapped or weighted down with obligations, and then to discover that it is also possible to feel honored to have that responsibility—often without a single change in the outside situation itself. The new experience comes from an inner change of perspective. An unloving mate can easily turn from a frog into a prince if you begin to perceive him from a soul level and sense the inner radiance of his heart. A frog can also turn into a princess when someone truly sees her as a noble being of love in her Essence Self. (Struggle may feel like karma, but we guides see karma as merely one's deep belief that things are not yet in balance. If you feel it is your karma to struggle to survive or achieve, then it is—but only so long as this deep belief is present.)

As you realize your freedom to choose your life direction, you can see how important it is for you to give the people who are close to you the same freedom to choose their life directions. Your freedom to learn from your experiences and to take responsibility for each action opens your mind and heart to allow friends and family to take full responsibility for their lives as well. You may enjoy watching others discover the sovereignty of who they are, free to choose, learn from their choices, and choose again—just as you are doing. This is the path to mastery. If, for example, you see a better way for a friend to be successful, assume that he is learning precisely the skills that will most benefit him now. What you see is how you would handle the situation if *you* were in it. His skills and experiences are different than yours. But you can help him to see his choices more clearly by spinning a Bridge of Light to wisdom, bringing him onto this bridge, and allowing the pure light to permeate both of you.

LAUNA I*t is a profound truth that our experience of life depends precisely on the viewpoint we take— although the truth of this is much easier to see when we look at other's lives. We get the experience that matches our deep belief. A good example is that of a coworker who told me recently, "This is the year that I will experience abundance on* every level and get my work out there in the world." And indeed she did. Her seminars are reaching many people and assisting them to live far more joyfully. She is experiencing prosperity and abundance in her work. She believed in what she said because she chose it as her reality. And when someone believes in something, she sees that it happens. She is clear, committed, organized, focused, positive, and willing to forgo or postpone any other pleasure that would break that fine concentration and efficiency in her work. She is also willing to begin again and reorganize her office, her plans, her ideas, if they are not working efficiently and successfully. The one thing she will not compromise on is honoring her higher guidance.

Two years ago Dr. Linda Johnston, a physician, told me, "I want to be the best homeopathic doctor I can possibly be and spread homeopathy to patients and doctors throughout America and the world." She spent the money she made to study with the best teachers, often seeing thirty-two patients in her office each day in order to catch up with her patient load so she could continue traveling and studying. She began to eat and sleep while thinking of homeopathic remedies and to reflect on the right homeopathic remedy for each patient she was treating. She has taken the stance that she can make a powerful contribution to people's health and happiness through homeopathy, and she is constantly energized by rechoosing this stance. She is becoming an excellent homeopath, because she chose the stance that it was possible—and then dived in to make it happen. (See Appendix.)

On the first meeting of my weekend seminar, "Handling New Levels of Light," I ask the participants to imagine their lives five years in the future as they are enjoying the fruits of all the choices toward their highest purpose. Each participant then describes this life to the group in the present tense. For example, "I have established a center for young creative artists. We *have children coming to this center from all over the world who are amazingly creative." Gregory, one of the group members, is telling the group his vision as if it is happening now. The effect is very powerful on the person speaking. He realizes that everyone accepts without question what he is doing—even though he may be shaky about how he will ever do it. Suddenly, Gregory actually sees himself as the creator and director of this children's center. The choice to make his vision real becomes an actual possibility for the first time. It's even more powerful when people ask others about their new work. They describe how they got started, what blocks they went through to make it a success, and how deeply satisfying it is—without the slightest hint that it is in the future. After a while there is such an air of enthusiasm and confidence that people work in teams to plan details, to teach and learn from each other. They have anchored this new picture into their lives and they are going about making it happen in very practical, realistic terms. The knowledge, training, contacts, and ideas they already have in order to bring in the reality surprises them more than anything else as they begin to walk into the reality they have created and to help their partners to do the same.*

You may want to select some friends and practice this way of choosing your highest possible futures. When others say, "I always make poor choices about my work or my relationships," stop them and encourage them to say, "I used to make poor choices about my work and my relationships. As of this moment I am making excellent choices through my higher intuition." It may be necessary to remind yourselves many times that each of you has the innate freedom—and the ability—to choose a new self-image and a new future, but it may be the most productive work you have ever done together.

Start now. Choose one specific belief to take about your life and during the next week repeat it over and over until you establish it into every neuron of your brain. Watch what hap-

pens as your ability expands to believe your new choice of futures.

EXERCISE
EXPERIENCING LIGHTED CHOICES

1. As you approach your temple, create a quiet mind so that you can decide wisely what you wish to take responsibility for. Imagine that on the front door, beside your name, is carved the phrase, "Freedom to Choose," and walk through the door into your temple. Think of how inherently free you are in mind, spirit, and body, aware that no one can control your life without your agreement.

2. Look at each responsibility and see if it is from your free choice—and if it fits your personal philosophy now. Choose the commitments that stem from your deep heart knowing.

3. Create a triangle of light to one situation that needs adjustment as a result of a stance you have taken about your responsibilities and your freedom. One point of the triangle of light will be from your heart, one from the wisdom within your head, and the third point in the situation itself.

4. Breathe in with full trust the power and love of your God within. The lines of light flowing through this triangle carry a tremendous power to transform the situation. See fine luminous strands of light pouring into your triangle. Say to yourself:

"I am free, I am free. I am free. I am free to live from the wisdom and the authority of my divine self."

"I am free to fully engage in the responsibilities that are mine and to experience joy over worry, love over fear."

5. Repeat these statements again and again until all the parts of your personality accept the idea, and old beliefs which prevented your expanding joy and effectiveness lose their momentum.

6. Imagine that each of your chosen commitments is being

energized and that the results are exactly as you are picturing—
positive and powerful in adding light to your life and the lives
of others.

Each time you think of this triangle of light, it becomes more
potent to transform the situation at hand. Many new options are
likely to appear in your mind over the next few days after you
form this triangle of energy. The luminous strands of light that
you spin can give you a very clear picture of the new options
that empower you and your work.

16

FINDING AND EXPRESSING YOUR PURPOSE

LAUNA *H*ow do we know what our pur-
*pose really is? Once we know our purpose, how do we get
enough power and light to start on it now? And how can we
stop using so much of our time and energy in activities that
have little value to us? These are critical questions that many
people are asking themselves.*

JAIWA *T*here is so much light permeating
minds and penetrating body cells that for those who want to
assist, the dilemma is what to do with all the light. A century
ago, even a generation ago, it took years to tap into the light

because of the density of the earth, but so much is being brought to the earth planet now that it happens quickly—you tune to it, open to receive, and it comes pouring through.

You each reflect different aspects of the one great light.

You who are awakening to a greater purpose in being here on this planet can consciously choose to express the specific facet of light that is most magnetic to you. Perhaps you clearly see your purpose as developing a wise and complete understanding of life so that you can teach and illumine others. Or perhaps you sense that your purpose is to develop a deep, intuitive, loving understanding of people, so that you can nurture them and help them unfold their highest potential. If these purposes are close to your own, you may have already noticed how expanded your heart feels when you hear of someone's suffering, or how sensitive you are now to group suffering and deprivation. You may be feeling an intense desire to reach out to help and don't know where to begin.

Some of you may sense that your purpose is to serve God, or your highest ideal, with complete faith and utter devotion. Or it may be to live with commitment, true to your highest vision of what is right. Others may aspire to become dynamic, powerful leaders, serving the greatest good or working to liberate people from oppression. Or you may see your purpose as learning truth through deep thinking and careful reasoning. Others may be most fulfilled putting practical, progressive ideas into action and seeing them through until they are well established.

Once you decide on your purpose look for different ways to express it. For example, if you are intrigued by the possibilities of bringing conflict into harmony, you might choose to work through art, family life, science, or religion. The divine quality of harmony shines through each soul differently. Even when many people are expressing harmony through a single art form, say, sculpture, each produces unique results and reveals a different facet of harmony.

Suppose 1,000 people decided to express beauty through dance. Each one would create a rhythm and style to express his own highest vision of beauty, and because of individual training, culture, and personalities, the variety of dances would be endless. Each would carry another facet of light into a form, and all who witnessed each dance could open to greater beauty. Even a dance that the dancer performed alone could bring forth a unique quality of beauty that would then be telepathically available to all who tuned to its vibration.

You may find that you already are expressing your purpose very elegantly. A young woman from Maine was sent to me, Jaiwa, because she couldn't "find" her purpose. She was serving hundreds of other people by making tapes available of her inspiring musical recordings. She was already expressing her purpose in a powerful way. When she realized the ripple effect she was having as these friends copied her tapes by permission and handed them on to others, a beautiful, serene expression came over her face; she took a very deep breath, paused, and let out a great sigh of relief. She confessed that the tapes just seemed like fun and she thought that her "purpose" should seem like struggle and sacrifice.

It is far more energizing to choose one area of work that gives your life the greatest meaning and to begin focusing on that area than to try to cover several areas. Look first into the area where there is the greatest need in which you have developed knowledge and skills. For example, if you have experienced a great deal of conflict in your life, you have probably learned important skills in creating harmony out of conflict. You may be able to move quite naturally into facilitating and teaching skills of working in harmony to individuals, families, and other groups.

Once you are clear about your highest purpose, help will come to you from many directions. We guides often teach you at night when your conscious mind is still and your active mind is in a receptive delta state. New people will come into your life to help as well. They may come from every walk of life to teach you. Some will help you clear old beliefs that are unproductive, even when they do not realize what they are doing. Your old beliefs about the fate of the world dissolve because of your enthusiasm in new ideas and plans.

Test every choice you make, even small ones, and see if they reflect your life purpose. Waiting for a bus, cleaning up the kitchen, or shoveling snow off the drive—no matter what you are doing—try asking yourself, "What is the point of what I am doing right now? How does this fit into my larger purpose? If it fits, a hit of higher energy will flow through your body. Even if what you are doing at the moment is simply taking care of the mechanics of living, remember how this also supports your purpose. These activities are part of the responsibility of living on this planet as you expand your awareness and begin to express your real purpose. You can eat, sleep, work, play, and even laugh while you are simultaneously aware that you are absolutely on purpose.

If you have a period in which you feel ambivalent about what to study, organize, or do next in expressing your purpose, first leaning one way and then another, simply imagine your life ten years in the future as it might be with each choice. The sense of adventure, new discovery, and high energy may be much stronger in one picture than the other. Or go into your temple and mentally put one possibility in each hand and notice which hand feels tingling and warm. That will be where the energy is, and you can safely select the next step according to the greater sense or warmth of energy. Where your energy is, there will be your heart and your highest joy—both the closest companions to your purpose.

All who sincerely ask can connect with the power of a new vision to lift them into a higher flow of energy.

Every human being on this planet has a purpose and is needed. The spiritual guides who are working with humanity need every one of you, especially now, to help bring forth a new world order of freedom, of love, and of light. Choose a group to serve and find out the needs of these people so you can answer their needs with your radiant love, your light, and your practical knowledge and skills.

A high vision that reverberates with the heart and mind energizes you and draws you toward what you envision. As you connect your vision with this light, you may get a flood of new ideas. How do you choose the best one? How do you move forward to realize your vision? What can you do right now?

Here are some needs that will be showing up in humanity soon, and some ideas to serve those needs.

Beginning this year many people may be experiencing periods of confusion, pulled between the old beliefs and the new. Their emotions can create a fog that temporarily confuses their minds. You can serve most powerfully by increasing the radiance of your Bridges of Light so that others may join you on your bridge and receive the light, clarity, or compassion they need.

Perhaps you are already responding to these needs. Focus your love and energy not on the people who are resisting the new incoming waves of light, but on those who are open and searching, who have already realized that there is far more meaning to this life experience than the culture has taught. Whatever your vision is to help, when you reach out to others from your heart you are serving a great need.

Ask for a vision that matches the power and the light of your soul.

Your true vision will resonate with your desire to serve humanity, draw forth your inner truth, and strengthen your commitment. Too grand a vision must be cut into smaller chunks before it can be implemented. Too small a vision will leave you without inspiration or enthusiasm. We do not tell you what that vision should be. You are its sole creator. At first, you may get only a hint of it, or you may be puzzled by a symbol that comes to you, but each session in quietness and solitude assists you to discover another piece that is needed. Ask your higher self to make it more clear, to refine it, and to show you how to manifest it.

Give yourself several weeks of focusing, every few mornings writing a description of your highest possible future, checking to be sure it is in line with your higher purpose. Thinking of it often will excite something deep within. The preparation you have already done usually starts becoming obvious, even if you didn't know at the time why you were having certain experiences and learning certain skills.

Develop the skills that your vision calls for.

Writing will help you get very clear and organized with your thoughts and plans. It can also expand your contacts beyond those who live in your immediate area. Here is an opportunity for any of you to set personal ambition aside while you simply reach out with a message of the reality of the soul and the knowledge that is opened in the light. You can self-publish your messages or send them via the network of electronic global communications established so efficiently by the workers in that field.

Do not count on anyone coming in to furnish what is missing. This expectation has stopped more light workers than almost anything else; they miss the urgency to develop the skills that their vision calls for in order to actually manifest their vision. Learn the skill of making connections, organizing and getting people to work together, communicating by computers, and attracting money for higher purpose. These skills are critical in manifesting almost any vision. It isn't that you will be doing it singlehandedly, but the ability to understand and use money wisely is necessary in order to attract it; the skill to organize allows people to delegate and share responsibility. Be alert for people you can work with for your vision.

Think of the preparation as part of your purpose as you prepare more thoroughly to fully express this vision. But beware of delaying your teaching or healing indefinitely out of false humility. If you wait until you know everything there is to know about your field of work, or for more money to come, or for the right partner or your true teacher, your part in the great work for transformation might sit on the sidelines for years while you are preparing to express it.

Become an expert in your major field of interest by focusing totally on it for a period of time. What is on purpose for one person may be a distracting, off-purpose activity for another. Your vision may be one of working to achieve healthier physical bodies while someone else's path is to work for children's rights. Someone working to establish laws to protect the environment could be spreading his energies too thin by also working to free global political prisoners. If you are working with alternative schools or to bring a higher wisdom into form, working in nutritional research could be off purpose for you. It is important to establish yourself in the field that you are most strongly attracted to even if you have a strong interest in several.

Build a Bridge of Light to wisdom or clarity. Let its energy flow into any problem area that is presenting a block to your vision. Ask your Higher Self, "How can I use this situation to further my highest purpose?" New ideas may suddenly seem obvious and offer you choices that were not available to you before. The ideas you contact from your bridge are a direct connection to how to make your vision happen.

Spend your time as consciously as you spend your money. Each week you have exactly 10,080 minutes. The richest, most powerful person in the world has not one minute more. Ask yourself frequently, "Is this the best use of my time?" Put this question on cards and keep one by the phone and one in every room of your house, your automobile dashboard, and your office. Within a few weeks your time will seem to expand quite magically.

Think of your future as one of increasing levels of joy. The idea that expansion comes through suffering and that service comes only through dutiful sacrifice is no longer appropriate for the higher vibration of energies. The new keynote of this planet is *joy*. Reflect deeply on the joy that might be possible in your vision until you have a feeling of expansion in your head and your heart.

EXERCISE
FINDING YOUR PURPOSE

Choosing the purpose which most clearly resonates within your heart and mind adds meaning and joy to your life. Take a few minutes to become so clear that you can describe it in just a few sentences even though you may already have a sense of it.

Take three sheets of paper and copy one of the questions below at the top of each sheet. Then sit in silence and calm your mind. It's helpful to let go of the day's focus on work and let a sense of serenity permeate your body. Move into the luminous inner sanctum of your Temple of Light. Experience the silence, establishing a deeper channel through which to see the true purpose of your life. Then answer these questions.

1. What do you want to know and understand more than anything else in the world?
2. What is of the greatest value to you on this planet?
3. What vision causes your heart to open and embrace all life?

These answers will help to reveal your life's purpose.

If you are not truly inspired by your sense of purpose, imagine that you have exactly nine full and healthy months of life left on this planet to express the most important thing in your life. Plan what you would do in those nine months. What could you do right now that would meet the needs of some groups of people?

EXERCISE
FULFILLING YOUR VISION

It's one thing to know your purpose and another thing to actually begin to take action on it now, or to expand the action you are already taking—and to do it with real joy. Here are the steps that Jaiwa and I present to people in the Bridge of Light seminars. Before you go into your temple for this exercise gather a sheet of paper and a pencil or pen.

Sitting in the main room of your temple, tune to the vibration of your purpose, the power and the beauty of it, until you feel its vitalizing energy. Make this feeling the basis of your vision for the future.

Imagine how you will feel, how your life will be different, and what you will see when you manifest your vision. The vision doesn't need a rigid form at this stage while you are gathering new energy and stability. If your vision is capable of taking you to your highest possible future, you will feel a definite stimulation in your heart as you think of it.

Create a movie in your mind of yourself walking into a room where you will learn what you need to know. See yourself with a smile on your face and a book under your arm as you open the door. If you can step into your movie and actually experience the weight of the door as you open it and your delight as you walk into the room and take a seat at the front, the results are quicker.

As you walk into your movie keep in mind your higher purpose of being a healer, a teacher, a scientist, an educator, a communicator, a writer. This moves you into a vibratory pattern that joins you with all the true servers—your own kind of people—who give with an open heart and share their understanding, knowledge, and resources whenever possible.

Imagine the immediate, practical steps you can take to show your higher self that you are serious. You may be surprised at how much you can do now. A phone call, a letter, a friend, or a group contact may be the very first step. Schedule time for taking this step within the next five days. Write your intention on a sheet of paper.

Remember, it is not only *what* you are doing, but the experience of delight and discovery that marks a life of true value. When you remember that you already are a being of light and of love, you can touch the joyous peace that is always available to you. Then any direction in which you move to fulfill your purpose will bring joy and fulfillment.

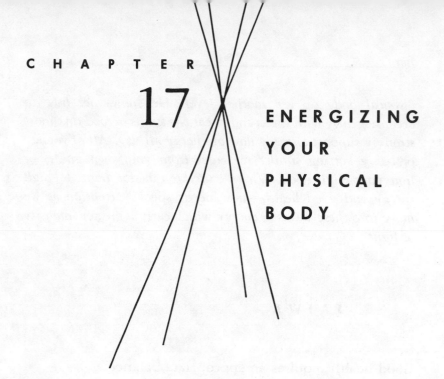

CHAPTER 17

ENERGIZING YOUR PHYSICAL BODY

LAUNA In the seminars I am teaching, the participants often ask Jaiwa why they are having physical aches and pains that have no medical cause. They want to know how to get more physical energy and maintain an alert mind for their work. Opening to the light makes demands on your physical body that weren't there before. When new light begins to move through you, your body's nutritional and other needs are stepped up tremendously. We can also greatly benefit by strengthening the light bodies that are closely interwoven with our physical bodies so that we have greater protection from both disease and negative energies.

One of my closest coworkers, Sanaya Roman, who has been channeling many excellent books, has been instructed by her wise guide, Orin, at each stage of her expansion to bring her

physical body up yet another level. He shows her how to
exercise gently with walks and to eat the kinds of food that most
strongly support a steady flow of energy all day. All of you are
probably getting similar messages from your own guides or
from your Higher Self. What we used to take for granted—high
energy and good health—now needs special attention as we
move into these waves of energy which carry a greater intensity
of light.

J A I W A

Good health requires an appropriate balance.

To maintain good health requires a balance of meditation,
purposeful activity, good companionship, music, and color. For
optimum health do a mental review at the end of each day to
release the tensions from the mind. Your emotions and your
physical vitality are closely tied together. As you clear the
energy in one, there are always positive benefits in the other.
With a good diet, exercise, and ample sleep, your physical body
will be stronger and serve you better.

All the powerful inner work you are doing—creating visions
of your best possible future, spinning Bridges of Light, teaching
your subpersonalities how to cooperate with your purpose—
makes extra demands on your body. The expansion that is
taking place in your mind and your emotions calls for an equal
upgrading of the cells in your body, including the cells of your
brain. Your body may already be more sensitive to low-quality
substances, especially junk food, alcohol, or drugs. It may be
reacting to fraudulent foods that look and taste like food but
offer no nutritive value. If so, it will waste no time in telling

you so by initiating a slowdown or a time-out for recovery when you do not honor its new needs.

Study the new information available about keeping your body in top physical shape, slowing the aging process, and enjoying a clear mind. Choose foods and drinks which contain life energy. Food that is natural and fresh has an essence value as well as high nutritional value. When you eat it your body can resonate more easily with the higher energies you are discovering.

In addition to the food you eat, you are also nourished by something that is invisible to the five senses. This nourishing element is the life spirit which enlivens all forms—human, animal, plant. Each time you go into your Temple of Light, your physical body consciousness is awakened to a higher potential of vitality and health. In order to stay in harmony with the increasing vibration of light and to handle your increased sensitivity, your body needs to step into a finer vibration as well.

You feed your body with the light of your inner sun.

Each day in your Temple of Light imagine new cells of greater vibrancy replacing old ones. As you breathe slowly and deeply your thoughts of light will attract lighter, healthier cells to your body. Physical and emotional healing are promoted when you have an abundance of the slower brain waves magnifying your focus on harmony.

If you experience discomfort as you handle new waves of light surging through your body, mind, and emotions, notice what you feel and where you feel it, and you can correct any imbalance. The work you do in your temple is helping your body to flush out accumulations of toxins from years of eating food with little life essence. As these toxins are routinely flushed, they won't stack up and cause sluggish feelings. Be glad to have the opportunity to clean out accumulations which are not in harmony with your spirit. The greater light is restoring your body, keeping it young and flexible.

The more you meditate and call in the light, the more important it is for you to know how to distribute that light. Otherwise you could create a congestion of light in your head. If constriction builds, your head might feel tense around the back near your neck. If this happens, it is a signal to reconnect all the pathways of light running through your body. Distribute the energy through your body and out to the world by visualizing light and love streaming forth into the minds and hearts of all humanity.

If you do a lot of work with your hands, writing or healing, you may find some of the energy is congesting in your arms and shoulders. The secret is to keep the energy moving. Move your body frequently, not in familiar automatic patterns but in graceful and open free-form movements. Free-form dancing to beautiful music alone or with others is very energizing and balancing to your body.

You are developing a radiant body as you distribute the light of your temple through it. The closer you are in touch with your life spirit from moment to moment, the more beautiful and radiant your body will become. An expanding beauty is the inevitable result of consistently feeding your body with inner light.

You can reinforce your light body and build extra immunity.

The body of light that interpenetrates and surrounds your physical body is the key to your physical health. It receives and transmits higher energy to your physical body when it is strong and vital. You may actually feel lighter and more graceful as light is woven into it. Your body of light helps protect you from illness as it restores your energy field after stress. Hostile take-overs by viruses are stopped on its outer edge unless it is weakened in some way.

You also have the ability to sense an approaching disease. You may not "see" as some clairvoyants do, but you can sense a weakened light body with your intuition, as you would sense a hole in your coat if the cold air was blowing on you. Sharpen your sensitivity to the whispered warnings. These will always come when you are out of balance with nature, not exercising enough outdoors, and eating or sleeping without respect for your body's genuine needs.

As you strengthen your body of light, it will extend farther away from your physical body. You strengthen it by using your creative imagination. Mentally weaving lines of lighted energy around your body is a powerful way to build a greater field of energy that can expand to thirty feet or more. You can do this every day until you sense your optimum vitality returning. You can then reinforce your protection and expand the radiance of your light body by a few moments of visual-izing lighted lines of energy going through your body. At the end of the chapter you will find a process for strengthening the light body.

LAUNA *There are so many excellent re-sources for you to draw on, it is worth mentioning some here.*

A few people seem to have come to the planet at this time specifically to help people make the physical transformation into more light through untangling the streams of energies in their subtle bodies. Dr. Duane Packer is one of the gifted healers who is teaching people how to see these patterns and to detect disturbances in the light body before they are felt in the physical body. He is currently writing a book on how to make changes in the subtle energy bodies so they can hold more light.

Other people are researching the nutritional needs created by spiritual awakening. They use their training and intuition to find ways to help raise the vibration of the body at a cellular level so that it can keep pace with an accelerated movement into light. One of these people is Gabriel Cousens, a holistic physician and nutritionist who teaches and writes about spiritual nutrition. His book, Spiritual Nutrition and The Rainbow Diet, presents a blueprint of the nutrition necessary for creating more conscious people to help transform the planet into a peaceful, loving world. Particularly helpful is his clarification of the live food concept and how the processing of food affects consciousness and energy.

There is much validated research on preserving and restoring the vitality of the physical body. The accelerated stress factors can be counteracted by the newer discoveries in nutrition. You might start with a nutritional analysis of your diet that gives you a detailed report of any missing nutrient and indicates what foods supply this nutrient. This may be more useful than simply buying supplements without an individual chart. (See Appendix.)

The Alexander technique is taught all over the United States. The teachers can help you to reconnect the lines of lighted energy where they have become disconnected or congested. They never say do this instead of that, but help you to see what you are doing that is interfering with your natural body flexibility. Alexander teachers point out the integrity of movement in a healthy child and show how we lose it by imitation of others or by trauma, and then, out of habit, continue using our bodies in the patterns imposed over the original integrity. We push the neck forward and the head pulls back. This compresses the front of the body. The hips go forward and the knees and ankles are stressed, much as in the gunslinger or model stance. But trying to do something different won't work. When we try to get rid of this imposed pattern, we tend to arch our backs and lift our chest. Muscles collapse or grow rigid, losing tone and the balance which comes from free and lengthened muscles and free, open, and flexible joints.

The body is much lighter when it is free of all this imposed pressure. Freedom in the muscles and joints allows flexibility. Our highest potential for free joints and lengthened muscle balance keeps shifting. The tension necessary to move a muscle is incredibly minute. Our culture teaches us we must tighten and shorten muscles in order to move, which causes rigidity as we get older. We take for granted that the way we move is the right way and forget that flexibility could be natural throughout our lives.

All of the original Alexander teachers are in their seventies and eighties and are still teaching as well as riding horses and gracefully moving about the world. Their ability to listen, to observe, and to communicate reveals their intellectual clarity and ability to observe on many levels at once. They emphasize that this ability is not unusual but innate within all of us.

In the Appendix you will find the address to inquire about an Alexander teacher near you. I find these sessions very powerful. Even when I think nothing is happening, my body tells me differently afterward. All of us can learn to become trained observers of our bodies. With a simultaneous touch of our fingers and sense of compassion from our hearts we can often release unconscious patterns that are holding the memory of a shock or trauma.

Homeopathic remedies also work on the subtle body of light to restore its optimum condition so that the whole person can be healed, rather than work only on the physical body. Homeopathy is now being made available through a few physicians and others who have gone through years of training in order to learn *this highly sophisticated science of healing. With over 2,000 remedies, each one affecting simultaneous changes in the emotional and mental self as well as the physical self, amateur dabbling is not recommended. Even though the substance of these remedies is from plants and herbs, the effect can be quite potent. Knowing which one to use, when to use it, and what potency to use is of utmost importance. (See the Appendix for reference address.)*

The Bach Flower Remedies represent an alchemical fusion of the spiritual essence of the flower in cooperation with the emotional and mental needs of the person. They are not used directly for physical illness, but are extremely effective when someone is fearful, irritable, apathetic, depressed, guilty, hopeless, jealous, revengeful, suspicious, and a host of other things. There are thirty-eight flowers which Dr. Bach discovered to cover every negative state of mind. He classifies them under seven major headings: apprehension, indecision, loneliness, insufficient interest in circumstances, oversensitivity, despondency and despair, and over-care for others. The remedies appear to work with the life force, allowing it to flow freely through or around the block and speed healing. These flower remedies are ideal for self-use. (See the address in the Appendix for supplies and information.)

EXERCISE
FREEING THE BODY FOR FLEXIBLE FEELINGS

Each position in which you sit, lie, stand, or walk is associated with a certain emotion or a series of emotions. By putting your attention on your body, you can observe which feelings and memories are triggered by various positions. One way to do this is to pose your body in a position of fear. Make this position as extreme as you can. Once you have captured the drawn face, clenched hands, and tense muscles, hold the rigidity for one minute. Notice your breathing in this position, and the tone of thinking that runs through your mind, even though you have voluntarily taken this position.

Now put your body in the exact opposite position, one which feels free, joyous, balanced, strong, and centered. Breathe in this position. As you inhale, your body is refreshed and made fragrant again. By taking several breaths in this position, you will begin to feel joyful and loving. Notice your thoughts, your identity of yourself, your level of confidence, and your spirit of compassion.

Resume the first position for ten seconds, and the second for ten. Alternate these opposite positions several times, and you will begin to see the power of your physical posture to bring in a happy mood and an energized body very quickly.

EXERCISE
STRENGTHENING YOUR BODY OF LIGHT

Each cell in your body has its own aura. In the following exercise imagine that you are creating more space for each cell. When cells are not nourished with sufficient light from your energy field, it is as if they are squeezed and contracted. They flourish when their auras have abundant space and nourishment. In this exercise you will also be flushing dense cells out of your body and inviting new ones with a higher vibration to replace them.

Lie on a mat with your head flat and relax for a few minutes, breathing deeply before you begin the exercise.

Imagine a star six inches above your head. Slowly bring its light into your head—into your left brain, your right brain, and your forebrain.

Now focus all of the light at the base of your brain, just above the first vertebra in your neck. Imagine that it is forming lighted lines of pure energy.

Beginning at the base of the brain, imagine these lines of light moving through the vertebrae of your neck. Let them permeate the space between vertebrae in your spine, one vertebrae at a time. You are lengthening your spine as you do this and rebalancing your nervous systems, both the sympathetic and the parasympathetic.

Next, bring the lines of energy out to each shoulder and down to your elbows, then connect them to your wrists and fingers. See a double line of lighted energy on the front and a double line on the back of each arm.

Begin again at the shoulders, this time bringing a line of this potent energy of light along each side of your torso to the large muscles in your hips.

Now mentally extend this light down the front of your legs, to your knees, then to your ankles, and into your feet and toes.

Repeat the process on the back side of your shoulders, your back, hips, legs, and feet.

If you still feel tense or fatigued, add a diagonal line beginning at each shoulder and ending at the opposite hip. This will reinforce your invisible armor and assist the balance between your shoulders and hips.

Imagine that each muscle and organ in your body is a member of a great symphony orchestra and that you are the conductor watching it respond to your baton, and listening to it resound in harmony with the universal energies.

By strengthening and reinforcing the network of lighted lines of energy around your body, you can be prepared for any situation. Negative energy coming to you from the outside will either be sent back to the person who sent it or absorbed in the light and transformed. You can feel confident each night as you go to bed that you are protected from the crosscurrents of negative energy that are going through the airwaves. Even unconscious parts of yourself will be attracted to this light and bathe in it.

JAIWA

A Celebration of Your Life Force

You are a radiant being of light. Celebrate who you are by this journey into truth.

Ask your body's forgiveness for any abuses—not exercising, or eating poorly, or creating stress that blocked its smooth energy flow. Have a conversation with your body and make a commitment to fulfill its needs for play, rest, nutrition, and life spirit.

Feel the face of a flower with your fingers. Now cup your own face in your hands with the same tender compassion.

Touch your body. Run your fingers lightly over the surface of your skin. Gently stroke one arm, beginning with your shoulder and moving to your fingertips. Notice how much longer the stroked arm feels. Your attention and the healing energy in your fingers releases each arm from a subtle contraction. When you think of your body, become aware of the incredible power and love of the life force which created it. See it as your luxurious mobile home giving you a place out of which to work, to love, and to play on the planet.

Touch others whom you know and care about in the same way that you would reach out to touch the beauty of a rare orchid or a bright yellow rose.

If you feel fatigued or low in energy, stand up and walk outdoors. Whatever the weather, select a place to walk and feel the magic of your steps on the ground. Breathe in the fragrance of the life energy of plants and trees by touching them as you inhale. You can receive a transfusion of energy by standing close to a tree and putting your arms around it. Since the essence of a tree is light, its pure energy is available if you open your heart and your arms to receive it. As you become sensitive to this subtle energy, you can actually feel the charge going into your body.

Watch or hold a puppy, a kitten, or a child in your arms to remind you of the wonderful flexibility that is natural to your body.

Construct in your imagination a luminous cape, a white cape with a hood that is long and flowing. You are a worker in the light; you may as well wear a cape that is made of light as you walk on this planet.

With your white cape flowing, hold your arms up and out from your body and turn your palms upward. Release a message of light or love to all the people on this planet. See them beginning to awaken and create their own capes of luminous light as they stand resplendent in vitality and joy.

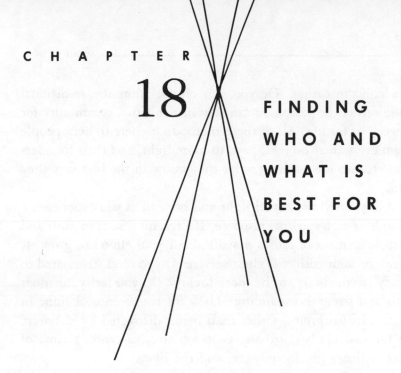

CHAPTER

18

FINDING
WHO AND
WHAT IS
BEST FOR
YOU

LAUNA *O*ur *expansion of consciousness can happen more rapidly at this time than ever before as we discriminate between who and what is right for us among all of the new-age teachers, ideas, innovations, and claims. But who has time to check out all the material now available in tapes, videos, books, seminars, and classes? A teaching can be excellent for some people and yet not be helpful to others at this juncture of their path.*

JAIWA You can choose from a vast array of tapes, seminars, spiritual groups, books, newsletters, and academic institutes. Or you can choose from the traditional religions of the past. You can stay in a spiritual community for a week or for life. All of these methods are here to help people from every stage on their path to more light, and their founders and creators are teaching what they know in the best way they can.

Ask yourself if you feel light and hopeful as you experience a sample of each spiritual resource. If a teaching adds to guilt and discouragement or causes despair about your efforts to grow, it is not on your path of highest service. Do you feel stimulated to study, to meditate, to be more loving? Do you feel your inner will and strength expanding? Look for the essence of light in each spiritual group, rather than being distracted by elaborate or unusual clothes, rituals, exotic centers, accents, claims of extraordinary psychic powers, and the like.

What about teachers? You may find a teacher who speaks with eloquence and who has studied for years, yet only your left brain is stimulated. As you listen to this kind of teacher lecture, you tend to take notes and make outlines and lists. Look for the teacher who speaks simply and who speaks from his or her own experiences and training. Out of that experience may come the *blending* of the lights of wisdom and love so that one powerful beacon shines forth and makes a lighted way for each student.

These teachers leave you free to choose the rules in your life that represent your expression of the light within you. And they so stimulate the white flame of your soul that you will be drawn more strongly than ever to be close to that flame, to know its purpose, and to set up your life so that you can follow it.

Discipline imposed from the outside is not as useful as that which comes from the love of your heart for the vision that your Higher Self has presented to you. If the instructions from a book, tape, or teacher continually seem burdensome and you do them *only* as a duty or obligation, perhaps that particular practice or exercise is not on your higher path. In any teaching, choose what resonates within you and inspires your highest truth. If a subpersonality is reluctant to cooperate with your true spiritual expansion, however, you can take it to the temple and gain its cooperation.

LAUNA *If you desire to choose a spiritual teacher, here are a few suggestions and questions that I have learned to answer very carefully from my intuitive mind and my rational mind before I plunge into anything.*

- *Watch for the essence of the message. Does it ring with the truth that is in your heart?*
- *Listen very carefully to the voice, the tone and the quality of each teacher. Close your eyes and see what you feel within from the energy field of this person.*
- *Look at the teacher's intention. What is the vision? How does this person or group carry out their plans—by purely voluntary action based on a will to good, or by pressure or subtle promises?*
- *How inclusive are the beliefs presented? Do they acknowledge the validity of all religions or join with other spiritual groups for wide cooperative efforts?*
- *Is the appeal to others' personal ambitions for power, status, or things? There is nothing wrong with this appeal; it simply does not satisfy the heart. The hunger in the heart must be filled first.*

You may desire to work with a therapist in order to bring your personality into a finer integration so that you may align it more easily with the soul's energy. It is important to select someone who not only is aware of the reality of the Higher Self, but also is in touch with and closely aligned to his or her own

Higher Self. Otherwise you may find yourself caught in a long process of studiously searching through the past in order to find reasons for problems. The logical mind can always find reasons, but very rarely are the reasons authentic. Once you are choosing light in your life, the solutions to personality problems can come from the wisdom of the soul.

Your brain is very important to your expansion as the mediator and translator between your higher mind and your conscious mind. The most helpful resources and materials increase our understanding of who we are and open the door for us to see more of the vast palace of our true self. There are many electronic tools, such as the new "brain machines" coming into the market that stimulate dormant brain cells and help to synchronize the left and right sides of the brain.

Also consider various "brain-tune" audiotapes with either the binaural beats (a different frequency in each ear) or a controlled echo from one ear to the other, which can produce powerful and rapid changes in your state of consciousness. Robert Monroe, founder of Hemisynch, has produced a number of these tapes that are excellent. He is the pioneer in creating out-of-body experiences for people through audiotapes. MSH association has produced others which have an intrinsic beauty and a very calming, peaceful effect on the mind and body as you listen. Both of these sets of tapes employ ways to take you into a slower brain-wave pattern and to synchronize the brain waves. The advanced programs offer much deeper experiences for meditation and exploration of altered states of consciousness. See Appendix for addresses.

Some musicians and composers have been able to tune to the music of the spheres and reproduce some of its magic with the aid of electronic devices, as well as through the angelic sounds of the flute, pan pipes, harp, and violin. Nearly all of the orchestral instruments can help to heal and restore a harmonized emotional field around you. Choose the ones in which you feel the most expanded as you listen. Include the classics. Each of them has brought a specific gift of expansion to humanity—on the emotional plane (Beethoven), the mental plane (Bach and Mozart), and the spiritual plane (Wagner). There are many others.

To find the seminars and workshops that will serve you best, notice the feeling you have almost immediately as you begin to read the description. You will become more and more sensitive to this level of inner knowing. It does not depend upon the sophistication of the presentation or the claims made of the results. You will find that an inner message can come to you. It will say, "This is the one," or else "Wait, not yet." Check for outer confirmation by calling and talking to the sponsors or to the presenter if that is possible. You can tell a great deal about the level of awareness and integration on which the approach is made by the voice and tone as well as the words of the people involved. If you immediately sense the energy of the heart combined with the wisdom of the head, you can probably trust the awareness work offered. Heart energy alone tends to be sentimental and one-sided; head energy alone tends to be separative and cold; but the two together are dynamite for creating the atmosphere in which people can accelerate their growth into more light. Once you have chosen, decide that you are going to gain from every moment, and you very likely will. Part of the pleasure is the opportunity to know and be with a group of souls who, like you, have been drawn to that teaching.

JAIWA

Performing some type of service offers a rapid integration of the light that is moving through you. It gives you the opportunity to use all the energies that you have contacted from your temple and Bridges of Light. Some of you think you have very little to offer, but we suggest you reassess your skills, your attributes, and your experiences. You may find that you really do have the knowledge, the understanding, and the Tools of Light to form small groups and meet for the purpose of bringing a greater light into this planet.

When a few people are gathered together, there is an exponential rise in the energy that can be channeled through the group from higher sources. That energy can be sent according to your direction. You can form a small group to receive energy from the telepathic sending and receiving room of the temple and then send that energy out to some group—the children of the world, the world leaders, the teachers, the parents. Or you can send it to all of humanity. Choose a regular time, once a week or once a month. If you gather for an hour or so you will find that the energies flowing through you bring a new surge of power for other work as well.

Look for the books, the tapes, the music, the group, or the teacher that speaks to your heart and helps you to feel expanded and loving. Listen for the song within your spirit and create dances between love and wisdom, courage and confidence, harmony and beauty, truth and trust, joy and intuition. These soul qualities are the beacon lights that attract the people, the work, the travels, and the adventures that will satisfy your purpose here.

There are many rays of wisdom which have not yet entered fully into this planet. If you can imagine how expanded the thinking soon will be—beyond anything known today—you sense the ongoing adventure of expansion. Every year you can touch upon greater truths that carry more light than present ones. As you embrace new insights brought by the greater light, you can also grow through love.

Why not dance into your future, laughing and playing with the universal energies of love, enjoying the common frailties in all of humanity, forgiving even though there is nothing to forgive, singing the songs that bring shivers running up your spine with their inherent harmonies of pure beauty? You can live and laugh and learn far more easily than ever before. Don't let anyone tell you that you are not expanding when your heart is filled with joy and your voice is filled with a song of love.

We guides watch your auras expand with joy and we rejoice with you. When you walk in such light, going in and out of your temple at will, spinning Bridges of Light to every facet of the rainbow; when you are willing to receive telepathically and send all that you have received out to the world you manifest the higher purpose of all spiritual training.

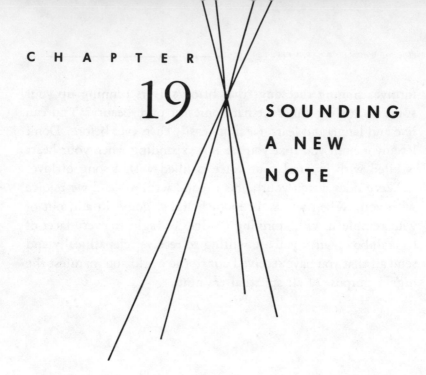

LAUNA I t may seem difficult for you to find time alone as the pace of life speeds up. You may be involved in family, work, or community activities day and night. Some of you may have to make appointments to spend time even with your intimate friends because you are leading such busy lives.

Jaiwa emphasizes how important it is to create some time alone each day in order to clearly receive the messages that are being broadcast from the higher planes. How can we get that time? And why is it so important?

JAIWA Y ou are in the midst of a transformation. You won't need to enclose yourself for the duration of this metamorphosis as the caterpillar does in its chrysalis—human transformation is made possible *because* of outside irritants as well as ecstasies. They are the catalyst for integrating greater light. But you do need a quiet space to clear your mind of all its distractions while you open your mind and heart to higher guidance. If you can't find a place to be alone during the day, you can awaken yourself in the middle of the night and spend an hour in the silence. Or you can arise in the early morning when a stillness of mind activity is still present in the atmosphere. If you can spend an hour before the world awakens, you may find that hour more valuable than two hours in the middle of the day.

There is an important reason why you need regular time alone. Your Higher Self is seeded with ancient symbols of greater knowledge and understanding. As you awaken and widen your channel to the Higher Self, the symbols will gradually unfold. They are going to be revealing many pathways—all leading to the great light. These symbols are set to be revealed to each person at exactly the right time. But it requires an inner and outer stillness to perceive them.

In any location, from a subway to a courtroom, with your active imagination you can create a special place of peace, such as a garden where there are fragrant flowers of all colors, or a meadow with the aroma of elderberry or peppermint, and peach blossoms. Or you can create a forest, cool and protected, fragrant with pine needles carpeting the earth. Go to the same place each time for restoring your harmony with nature. You can create beauty with your active imagination that feeds your soul, even in the midst of disturbing world events or personal disruptions.

If you want to become more radiant so that your energy field can be luminous and healing to the people you come into contact with, try spending some time alone in nature. The flowers, plants, and trees literally radiate a healing vibration because they are *always* in contact with light, especially the sun. Walking among the plants, you can regain a natural harmony, safely out of reach of most of the electrical and human broadcasts that go on in the cities. Soul-to-soul reception is natural when your only companions are living plants and animals.

In a quiet space outdoors under a tree, or beside a brook or lake, recall all of your life until now—your experiences, the most important lessons you have learned, your most developed attributes, and the strengths you are now developing. (When you are in your own home, section off a corner and set up a sacred space with incense, crystals, pictures that symbolize the master source of your life. Permeate it with the energy of your inner temple.) As you see how your life has been lived so far, where the emphasis has been and where the greatest joys have been, you can forget all about perceived or imagined mistakes. Each experience had an awakening value and led you to where you are now.

If you wish, you can unite with those guiding ones who know everything about you and love you without reservation. They give even though there is no way for them to receive. Turn to these beings and be willing to know them. From this companionship, a deep desire to give back may cause you to turn to another person, a group, or the whole race of humanity and offer what you can.

There is a rhythm in receiving from the greater light and giving that radiance to others. Tune into this rhythm and see which mode you are in right now. Some of you may have received all you can absorb of the light for now, and are ready to reach out to others. Others of you have given far too much without stopping to turn and receive. For you it is time to learn the art of receiving, to simply open to let in the healing love that the spiritual guides can offer to you. Many of you who are working with light are having difficulty knowing how to receive. You are so committed to giving, teaching, and healing, that at times you may forget how much is waiting for you to open to receive it. You can open these avenues by your conscious intention, by realizing that it is all right for you to receive from higher sources the reharmonizing and revitalizing that your mind and emotions and body must have in order to do the powerful work that you came here to do.

A Three-Day Experience in Nature

An hour or two in nature can make a large difference, but if you wish to cleanse your entire energy field, spend three days alone in nature. You can experience a deep level of communication with plants, trees, and flowers—even with birds and small animals. Whether you see them or not, they see you and can communicate to you when you are very still and peaceful. They too are expanding and evolving into higher consciousness.

The fresher the vegetation you eat, the more quickly you will clear the patterns for a higher receiving. If you can find food growing wild and eat it within an hour of harvesting it, your body receives its pure life force. Its vibration is so pure that when you bring it into your body in a spirit of gratitude, your vibration is raised. Try to do this with one food each day.

Become aware of a deep sense of peace. When you lay yourself open to a higher light free of interruptions for thirty-six hours or more, a healing pattern of light can move in and help dissolve blocks. In these three days, forget about time and all man-made pressures, and instead, fall into the natural rhythm of the changing sunlight, moving from dawn to dusk. Stop your activities when night falls, and gather strength from the stars. You may learn to see in the dark, to become aware of sounds you have never heard, to become alert to all the soundless rhythms of nature. Each time you enjoy such a three-day respite you can move into a new dimension of knowing yourself, releasing all that has happened till now and beginning again with fresh eyes and ears.

Receiving the radiant energy of the earth and the plant life is like being in your temple. Here you can connect telepathically with the souls in your own group. Or you may become aware of the fluid motion in your energy field as colors weave patterns around you. In such an atmosphere you may experience the kind of love and joy that seems to shoot out into the universe and then return to you, reverberating with a soundless touch. Whatever you can think of to send forth returns to you with twice the intensity.

During this time alone it is possible to connect with a sense of a greater plan to bring new light and love to this planet for the benefit of all of the kingdoms on earth—mineral, vegetable, animal, and human. You may get a sense of what you can do as you think of your purpose and your highest possible future.

Speak aloud to the power which represents the highest dimension of love and compassion for you. You might do this by sounding the name of Christ or Allah or God, or by using the names of any of the spiritual masters. There are 1,000 different names for God that are recognized around the world. Those which are alive for you will resonate in your heart and in your mind. You can use many of the names of God as the Sufis do, or use the one name that is sacred to you, and speak it aloud in your temple. Each has a separate sound and vibration that rekindles the flame of the soul.

Or you may simply realize how much you wish to open to greater light and to fully experience the unconditional love and joy it brings, knowing that you will naturally begin to radiate it out to others as you absorb it. If you want to add to humanity's potential for joy and for peace in some way—now is the time.

Here in the living energy of nature you can know yourself as we know you, and see that your shimmering essence is *you*—the real you. You may also see that the future you are creating is happening now. In this one endless moment your presence can pervade everywhere and everything. It can be a moment of bliss, of ecstasy and of peace, a timeless eternity of knowingness. Almost as if there is no experiencer, you can perceive and become one with the whole of nature and the whole of humanity.

You are now ready to integrate all your Bridges of Light into one grand Rainbow Bridge, radiating the colors of every spiritual quality. As you do this you will sound a new note, silent and powerful, reverberating in the hearts of all who can respond. The effect of your note will be felt wherever you go and through whatever you say and do. Let your note be pure, clear, and beautiful. Let it reflect the divine essence of your own soul.

FAREWELL FROM LAUNA

I want to tell you about a very powerful and effective way that I and many other people are using to sound our inner note and send its energy to others. Three of us form a triangle of energies. We imagine ourselves as points of light in a triangle form. The light flowing into us from our temples and bridges illumines each point of light as we visualize our triangle. The light then streams from each point and forms lines of lighted energy to connect the sides of the triangle. We then imagine our triangle interlaced with the thousands of other triangles formed by other groups of three all over the world as we speak aloud a special world prayer.

We take five minutes or so to visualize these triangles of light each day. Sometimes we may choose a specific group, such as the publishers and bookstores that are distributing new understanding and knowledge, or the metaphysical centers that are bringing together people of open minds and hearts. We visualize their light and power increasing throughout the world. Or we may visualize all the children of the world receiving the love and guidance they need before we include all of humanity as we say the world prayer.

The concept of these triangles comes from Lucis Trust of New York, Geneva, and London. There are apparently many thousands of triangles already formed around the world. On the spiritual planes these triangles are interlaced and form a powerful network of spiritual energy for humanity to draw from. The combined triangles create an open channel into human consciousness through which spiritual healing can flow and build a civilization of lighted minds and hearts.

If this idea resonates within your heart, I invite you to form a triangle of lighted energy with two other people and become a part of this networking from the spiritual planes. The three of you agree to send a message of love and light to humanity each day. To do this you first absorb pure light from your temple and imagine yourself as a point of light. You then visualize the other two people in your group as points of light in a triangle with you. There seems to be a geometric rise in power when a group of three are sending healing light and love, whether to a specific group or to all of humanity. Each triangle is illumined when one of you is visualizing it and directing its energy to humanity. The more frequently you visualize this triangle of spiritual energies, the more energy it carries.

With your triangle you can broadcast and distribute the higher frequencies of light and love each day at whatever time is convenient for you. When any member of your triangle visualizes it, each point is illumined and energized. The light of higher knowing, understanding, and compassion becomes available through these combined group broadcasts.

The world prayer that is being used to distribute the energy of these triangles is called the Great Invocation. It belongs to no religion or group and is known to be translated into more than fifty languages. (See Lucis Trust in the Appendix for requesting more information.) Every moment of the day or night someone or a group is voicing this invocation from somewhere on the planet. You may feel a deep response from within as you say it aloud and join the growing people like yourself who are finding deep joy in absorbing and distributing greater light.

THE GREAT INVOCATION

From the point of Light within the Mind of God
    Let light stream forth into the minds of men.
        Let Light descend on earth.

From the point of Love within the Heart of God
    Let Love stream forth into the hearts of men.
        May Christ return to Earth.*

From the centre where the Will of God is known
    Let purpose guide the wills of men
        The purpose which the Masters know and serve.

From the centre which we call the race of men.
    Let the Plan of Love and Light work out.
        And may it seal the door where evil dwells.

Let Light and Love and Power restore the Plan on Earth.

FAREWELL FROM JAIWA

We acknowledge you as a pioneer, courageously adventuring into greater light and service. As you and others like you bring your life into the finer vibration of your souls, a powerful sound goes forth, reverberating

*All the major religions expect a returning avatar or teacher. This teacher is known to Christians as the Christ, to Buddhists as the Lord Maitreya, to Muslims as the Imam Mahdi, to Jews as the Messiah, and to Hindus as the Lord Krishna. Each religion uses the name of its own expected one.

around the planet the note of pure joy that your souls send forth. The atmosphere is charged with the vibration of this harmonious sound. When there are enough of you who are sounding these new notes, the opposition to the right use of the life force will release its hold and all of humanity moves closer to the door of initiation into a higher consciousness.

Remember, it is not only *what* you are doing, but the experience of joyous discovery that marks a life of true value. If you embrace the peace and profound awareness that is always available to you in your temple, then any direction in which you move will bring you joy and fulfillment.

May every blessing be yours.

Jaiwa

APPENDIX

Audiocassette Tapes

A series of *Bridge of Light* audiocassette tapes by Jaiwa, through LaUna, of guided meditations in the Temple of Light, to many Bridges of Light and other Tools of Light in this book. These tapes use synchronized sounds and music to facilitate slower brain wave patterns and deeper meditation states. Write for listing of other tapes and free newsletter.
CHOOSING LIGHT, INC.
Box 5019
Mill Valley, CA. 94942

Guided meditation journeys by Orin as channeled by Sanaya Roman. These are excellent meditations that cover many topics. A quarterly newsletter is offered without charge on current earth changes and how to use the incoming energies.
LUMINESSENCE
Box 19117
Oakland CA 94619

Homeopathy First Aid audiocassettes offering a clear, practical, and safe use of first aid remedies in homeopathy and an introduction to the principles of Homeopathy.
LINDA JOHNSTON, M.D.
14624 Sherman Way, Suite 404
Van Nuys, CA 91405

Justine and Michael Toms have produced more than 1,000 excellent interviews of people who are on the leading edge of higher consciousness. New hourlong interviews are broadcast weekly on more than 200 radio stations across North America.

All of these programs are available as cassette tapes by mail order.
NEW DIMENSIONS RADIO NETWORK
Box 410510
San Francisco, CA 94141

Books

Bailey, Alice: Twenty-four volumes of the most complete esoteric
information yet offered to the public. A helpful volume is:
Telepathy and the Etheric Vehicle, E. V. Lucis Publishing, 1950.
LUCIS PUBLISHING CO.
113 University Place
11th Floor
New York, N.Y. 10003-4507

Cousins, Gabriel, M.D., A helpful book teaching four levels of
diet for enhancing the integration of spiritual energies.
Spiritual Nutrition and the Rainbow Diet.
Gabriel Cousins, M.D.
200 Spring Hill Rd.
Petaluma, Ca. 94952

Dossey, Larry, M.D. A visionary of broad understanding of
spiritual principles, Larry explores the concept of a mind
beyond the brain that is in touch with all minds.
Mind Beyond Body, Bantam, Spring 1989.
Beyond Time, Space, and Mecicine, Shambhala, 1984.

Ferrucci, Piero. One of the world's leading psychosynthesis
teachers writes of case histories with transcendent experiences
of clients and includes many exercises for experiencing the
Higher Self.
What We May Be, Tarcher, 1982.

Gawain, Shakti. A delightfully open approach to handling life's
challenges from her own experience.
Living in the Light. Whatever Press, 1987.

Hay, Louise. Powerful techniques for balancing a spiritual life and healing with self-forgiveness and love.
You Can Heal Your Life. Hay House, 1984.

Huffines, LaUna: A wise and gentle companion guidebook for *Bridge of Light* to help you discover the higher quality that each person in your life is teaching you. Includes a deck of sixty-four cards to draw from whenever challenges arise.
Connecting: With All the People in Your Life, Harper & Row, 1986. (Available only through Choosing Light.)

Hutchison, Michael. A fine exploration of the potentials of brain machines and other meditation tools.
Megabrain: New Tools for Brain Growth and Mind Expansion, Beech Tree Books, 1986.

Klimo, Jonathan. Offers a clear, intelligent and practical approach to understanding receiving impressions and knowledge from higher sources.
Channeling: Investigations on Receiving Information from Paranormal Sources, Tarcher, 1987.

Roman, Sanaya: Excellent books from Orin channeled through Sanaya Roman.
Spiritual Growth, H. J. Kramer, 1989.
Living With Joy, H. J. Kramer, 1986.

Roman, Sanaya, and Packer, Duane:
Creating Money, H. J. Kramer, 1988.
Opening to Channel, H. J. Kramer, 1987.

Periodicals

Magical Blend Magazine: Explores ancient and modern myths, magic and mysticism, charting the development of a new global age as society undergoes a fundamental transformation. Quarterly issues. Positive, insightful articles by some of my favorite visionaries.

MAGICAL BLEND MAGAZINE
Box 11303, Dept. J,
San Francisco, CA. 94101

Meditation: Supports people and organizations endeavoring to create a better world. A beautiful magazine full of excellent articles.
MEDITATION MAGAZINE
17510 Sherman Way #212
Van Nuys, Ca. 91406

Seminars and Workshops
Huffines, LaUna. Bridge of Light Seminar
CHOOSING LIGHT, INC.
Box 5019
Mill Valley, Ca. 94942.

Packer, Duane. Building a Body of Light and Clairvoyant Sight Training
LUMINESSENCE
Box 19117
Oakland, Ca. 94619

Roman, Sanaya and Packer, Duane. Spiritual Growth.
(Address above.)

Alexander Technique
AMERICAN CENTER FOR ALEXANDER TECHNIQUE
129 W. 67th
New York, N.Y. 10023

Bach Flower Remedies: Using the spiritual essence of flowers in

cooperation with the emotions and mental needs of the person.
DR. E. BACH CENTRE
Mount Vernon, Sotwell,
Wallingford Oxon OX10 OPZ, England

Nutritional Management Services: An excellent inexpensive
thirty-five-page computer-generated report with individual
analysis of your reported diet, identifying the missing or surplus
nutrients in your diet, and how to correct the deficiencies for
greater mental clarity and physical energy.
NUTRITIONAL MANAGEMENT SERVICES
Box 831990
Richardson, Texas, 75083

Alternative Travel Guide: Dianne Brause lists twenty pages of
organizations offering vacations that can fill the soul, make a
difference in your life and perhaps the lives of others. The list
includes adventure/sports, citizen diplomacy, cross-cultural ex-
changes, educational/language/study, environmental/ecology,
retreat centers, scientific expeditions/research, and volunteering/
work camps around the world.
ONE WORLD FAMILY TRAVEL NETWORK
P.O. Box 146130,
San Francisco, Ca 94114

Individual Transpersonal Consulting: St. Martin, Jean. Changing past memories, helping you to dissolve barriers and to live
with purpose and joy.
SANDHILL CRANE CLINIC
3626 N. Hall St.
Dallas, Texas, 75219

Music and Other Tools for Expanding Awareness

MSH Association offers many beautiful cassette tapes of music
to synchronize and slow brain waves to alpha and theta. A

four-year program called the Recognitions Experience and also residential programs are available by application.
MSH ASSOCIATION
Rt. 1, Box 192-B
Faber, VA 22938

HEMI-SYNCH: Robert Monroe has taken thousands of people through a series of week-long experiences of altered states of consciousness. The institute also offers a home course and individual tapes. The audiocassettes use binaural beats with headphones to facilitate out-of-body experiences for the participants. Robert Monroe is the author of *Far Journeys,* Doubleday, 1987.
THE MONROE INSTITUTE
Route 1, Box 175
Faber, Virginia 22938

Heavensong: Maloah and Michael Stillwater use harp, guitar, and their angelic voices to inspire the awareness of God within and to celebrate the awakening of the heart. They offer spiritual growth Summer Celebrations and retreats in Hawaii and other parts of the U.S. and audiocassette tapes of their music.
HEAVENSONG
Box 450
Kula, Hawaii 96790

World Service

Lucis Trust (Trust the Light) distributes Triangles information. Write for information on Triangles. The Arcane School, a seven-year course of study for steady spiritual awakening and developing true intuition, is offered by Lucis Trust.
LUCIS TRUST
113 University Place
11th Floor
New York, N.Y. 10002-4507

ADDITIONAL RESOURCES

Bridge of Light Tapes

To deepen your experiences of the Tools of Light offered in this book, Choosing Light offers several audio-cassette tapes. These tapes are guided meditations by Jaiwa—through LaUna—to facilitate the most effective results for you.

I offer these guided meditations and processes to you so that the gentle sounds of voice, beautiful music, and nature's harmonies may deepen your experiences in your Temple of Light and on your Bridge of Light. You will find yourself refreshed and revitalized each time you listen. (JAIWA)

Creating Your Temple of Light	BL10
Telepathic Receiving from Higher Guides	BL11
Bridge of Light to Joy	BL12
Bridge of Light to a Person	BL13

Tunnel of Light to Loving Understanding	BL14
Connecting With Your Soul Group	BL15
Magnetizing Your Highest Future	BL16
Meeting with Your Council of Elders	BL17

Each guided meditation in the group above is also enriched by stereophonic technology to assist you to synchronize your brain waves to Alpha and Theta ranges.

Other tapes for Integrating Light are:

Connecting Heart to Heart	CN10
Acting from Compassion	CN11
Connecting with Lighted Love	CN12
Connecting Beyond Giving or Receiving	CN13
Empowering Others	CN14
Experiencing Lightness and Humor	CN15
Radiating Inner Beauty	CN16
Living by the Authority of Essence	CN17

Each tape is $9.95 plus postage, and appropriate sales tax for California residents.

A complete set of these tapes in the Bridge of Light album is available for $49.95. The set contains four two-sided tapes packaged in a convenient cassette album. Add postage and tax per order form.

Write for a newsletter with updates on Tools of Light and new ways to use them for rebalancing and healing. It is offered without charge by request from Choosing Light, Box 5019, Mill Valley, CA 94942. Be sure to print your name, address, and phone number.

The book, *Connecting With All the People in Your Life,* by LaUna Huffines (Harper & Row, 1986, $14.95 Hardcover, 163 pp.) is available only through Choosing Light, Inc. It shows you how to connect from the heart regardless of the circumstances and includes a deck of 64 cards to draw from to see what each person is teaching you.

BRIDGE OF LIGHT SEMINAR: In a weekend in a beautiful mountain setting 45 minutes north of San Francisco, Jaiwa and LaUna facilitate new and joyous experiences of yourself which restore and revitalize your body, mind, and spirit. You will practice advanced techniques of each Tool of Light and meet people who are reflecting light in their lives.

RESIDENTIAL RETREAT: A one-week residential retreat near the mountains of northern California is offered annually for those who wish to experience a healing retreat into nature. In a rustic setting the impressions and guidance from your Higher Self or guide can come through you unhindered by the noises and energy blocks of the city. You will experience a new freedom to see how to activate your higher visions in a relaxed, joyful atmosphere surrounded by beauty, essence friendships, and times of silent reflection.

ORDER FORM

QTY	ITEM	DESCRIPTION	PRICE

Postage Rates: First Class U.P.S.

Subtotal

	First Class	U.P.S.
Up to $12	$1.45	$2.00
$13 to 25	$2.50	$2.50
$26 to 45	$4.25	$3.00
$46 to 65	$5.75	$3.75
$66 to 85	$7.25	$4.50
$86 to 100	$8.00	$5.75
Over $100	$10.00	$7.00

Sales tax*

Postage

Total

* CA residents add appropriate sales tax

Payment enclosed: **Check** **Money Order**

Your name: _____

Address: _____

City_____ **State**_____ **Zip**_____

Telephone: Home (__) _____ **Work (__)**_____

(In case we have questions about your order)

Make check payable to Choosing Light, Inc. Mail to Box 5019, Mill Valley, CA. 94942. Foreign orders need to be payable in U.S. funds. Canadian and Mexican orders add $2.00 to U.S. postage. Other foreign orders add $7.50 to U.S. postage.